LIBERATING

HOPE!

LIBERATING
HOPE!

Daring to Renew
the Mainline Church

MICHAEL S. PIAZZA AND
CAMERON B. TRIMBLE

THE
PILGRIM
PRESS
Cleveland

The Pilgrim Press
700 Prospect Avenue
Cleveland, Ohio 44115-1100
thepilgrimpress.com

16 15 14 13 12 11   5 4 3 2

Library of Congress Cataloging-in-Publication Data
Piazza, Michael, 1954–
    Liberating hope : daring to renew the mainline church / Michael Piazza and Cameron Trimble.
      p. cm.
    Includes bibliographical references (p.   ).
    ISBN 978-0-8298-1886-4 (alk. paper)
    1. Church renewal – Protestant churches. 2. Liberalism (Religion) – Protestant churches. 3. Church renewal – United States. 4. Liberalism (Religion) – United States. I. Trimble, Cameron, 1979– II. Title.
BV600.3.P53 2011
262.001′7 – dc22
                                    2011013105

Contents

Acknowledgments

One wonders if anyone actually ever reads the acknowledgment pages in books. Still, it is important to us that we acknowledge those who have been such an important part of this project and of the work we are doing through the Center for Progressive Renewal.

While the two of us get our names on the cover, and we get to travel around being the face of CPR, there is an incredibly competent staff and a dedicated board of directors that make it all possible. David Plunkett worked as long and hard on this book as we did. As our editor, he took the ramblings of two preacher types and tried to make them coherent and cohesive. He is the best when it comes to editing, but we try to keep it secret lest someone find out and pay him a whole lot more than we can. We want to thank Coy James, who contributed the chapter "Twenty-First-Century Stewardship." He has given this talk on behalf of CPR around the country, and many churches have found it most helpful. He is a wise and wonderful man and a dear friend. We also need to acknowledge and thank our many colleagues who have challenged us to think creatively about leadership in the church. These conversations have taught us, changed us, and opened us to new possibilities and hopes.

Of course, we both must acknowledge our respective spouses and families. On top of everything else we try to juggle in our lives, we have four teenage children between us. One of us has two sons, one in high school the other in college. The other has two high-school-age daughters. Fortunately, we also have wonderful spouses who handle our domestic lives, allowing us to be functional workaholics. They are the best.

Finally, we must say a word of profound gratitude to the United Church of Christ. While neither of us grew up in the UCC — we were both United Methodists — we have found the home of our hearts. The UCC's diversity, commitment to inclusion, and devotion to justice resonate deeply with who we are and what we believe church ought to be. We believe that is true with lots of folks who have found themselves outside the church looking for a home.

Much of this material was developed for our course "Seven Secrets of Renewal." So many people asked us for copies that we decided to compile it all here for them and others. We have written from our home in the UCC, though we hope the principles we discuss will apply to any mainline church that is seeking to be vibrant, vital, inclusive, and progressive. Thank you for taking this journey with us.

LIBERATING
HOPE!

Introduction

In 2008, the Broadway musical *Rent* closed after 5,123 performances as the eighth-longest running show in Broadway history. It is a show beloved by many, though the critics have not always been kind to Jonathan Larson, the show's creator. After the show closed, *New York Times* critic Charles Isherwood wrote about his experience of seeing the show when it opened and how its meaning changed for him in post-9/11 New York:

> One of the weaknesses of the show that bothered me a dozen years ago — the ending that finds the doomed Mimi springing back to life after appearing to expire — strikes me today as a flaw that Larson may have recognized but could not bring himself to correct. *The integrity of art must have seemed a less urgent priority than the dissemination of hope.* The awkward affixing of a happy ending to a fundamentally tragic story was a form of prayer, a plea that life might imitate art. I probably rolled my eyes at this absurd resurrection in 1996; this time I fought back tears.

We left high school, college or, perhaps, seminary with idealistic values and visions of a world waiting to be born. Along the way, though, we were exiled from those ideals and didn't do what we said we would. Today, as wizened cynics, we find those dreams to be all too quaint. Still, I believe that the *dissemination of hope is an urgent priority* that gives meaning to liberals living in exile. That is why we wrote this book, and I believe that is why you are reading it.

On a myriad of issues a significant number of Americans could be considered progressive, even liberal. In fact, in many

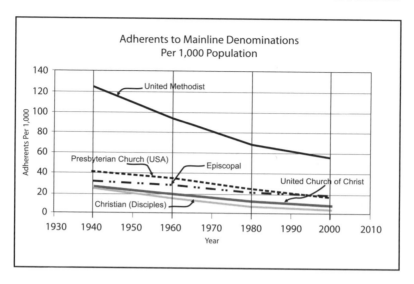

surveys, the majority would identify themselves as moderate to progressive:

- Climate change is viewed as a threat by 71 percent of Americans (Bloomberg Poll, September 10–14, 2009), and they want the federal government to address challenges such as global warming more aggressively (ABC News/Planet Green/Stanford University poll. July 23–28, 2008).

- An increasing number of people support marriage equality for same-gender couples (*www.marriageequality.org*).

- By a two-to-one margin, Americans favor reform to provide affordable health insurance to all (International Communications Research, September 16–20, 2009).

- The electorate has become increasingly progressive on social issues. Conservative politician are a small minority outside rural and southern areas, and even in those areas generational shifts are transforming the social landscape.

Given these facts, we are left to ask, "Why are churches and denominations that advocate these progressive values dying?"

Led by the Disciples of Christ and the United Church of Christ, mainline denominations are declining across the board.

Libraries of books have been written hypothesizing about the reasons for this decline. While we want to begin with a clear and accurate description of the situation facing the church today, this book seeks to offer concrete and tangible words of hope that these trends may be slowed and even reversed.

Our optimism is rooted in the Christian understanding of resurrection, but that is tempered with a wide range of experience in various church settings. We believe there is hope for the progressive church because we have personally experienced progressive churches that have been planted and renewed in some of the most conservative places. While we want to paint a realistic picture of the challenges that face progressive churches, we write this because of the signs of hope we see. This book is a conspiracy to persuade you to join us as believers in the hope that the progressive church can be renewed.

ONE

Expectant with Possibilities

On July 28, 2010, famous author and activist Anne Rice set off a firestorm of conversation across the nation when she wrote on her Facebook page:

> I quit being a Christian. I'm out. I refuse to be anti-gay. I refuse to be anti-feminist. I refuse to be anti-artificial birth control. I refuse to be anti-Democrat. I refuse to be anti-secular humanism. I refuse to be anti-science. I refuse to be anti-life. In the name of Jesus Christ, I quit Christianity and being Christian. Amen.

Within twenty-four hours she had more than 3,650 people "Like" her comment, and 1,820 people typed responses, mostly in affirmation, of her proclamation.

As it turns out, Anne Rice gave voice to what a lot of people were thinking. They love Jesus, but they have lost faith in the church. And who wouldn't? Because progressive people too often have failed to speak loudly or effectively in the face of bigotry, discrimination, and oppression on national platforms, the Christianity that most people think of stands against, rather than for, the positions about which moderates and progressives care most. Combined with mediocre Sunday worship experiences in too many of our mainline churches, Protestantism in America is in trouble.

In their book *Unchristian: What a New Generation Really Thinks about Christianity*, evangelical writers David Kinnaman and Gabe Lyons were shocked to discover that most young Americans perceive *all* Christians to be hypocritical, soul-saving, anti-homosexual, sheltered, judgmental political activists. While we as progressives can say, "Thank goodness this is not us," we have to acknowledge that no one would actually know that it isn't, because we too often abdicate our voice to the more conservative, radical, and outrageous among us. We are the "quiet" Christians, the ones who go to our historic Congregational, Methodist, Lutheran, and Presbyterian churches on Sundays, and in our own quiet ways we try to make the world a better place. We are moderates when it comes to most issues, and we value the neutrality that comes from walking down the middle of the road, rather than choosing one side. Our value of tolerance makes us reluctant to raise a counterpoint, even when religious fundamentalism threatens to blow our world apart.

This brand of moderation and tolerance worked well for us in the 1960s, when mainline Protestant churches were on every corner and the majority of the American population valued church attendance almost as much as baseball and apple pie. Church and the American culture were good and close friends. As time progressed, however, the mainline church became complacent, expecting that people always would sit in the pews voluntarily and sing the hymns of faith just as their parents had. Then American culture was rocked by the turmoil and social movements of the 1960s, which brought into question the formative norms of society, institutions, and, particularly, the church. Still, mainline churches had little concern about missional relevance or cultural perceptions, and few even noticed that the ministries that defined our churches were less and less aligned with the needs of our communities.

As American church culture shifted toward more rigid positions of *sola scriptura* and soul-saving evangelism on the right and pluralism and secularism on the left, the mainline church has tried to stay out of the fray. Trying to save the church from conflict, this decision created an atmosphere of spiritual malaise and cultural irrelevance and set the mainline on a path of decline.

After decades of growth and cultural dominance, the fundamentalist and evangelical churches today also are facing serious decline. While there is a fading perception that conservative churches are still growing — fed in part by a series of books published over the last twenty years with titles like *Why Conservative Churches are Growing* — the Southern Baptist Church is now among the fastest declining denominations in the United States. All measurements of vitality in the Southern Baptist Church are down, with the exception of a slight increase in baptisms in 2010. Even the Catholic Church is in trouble. According to a 2008 report published by the Pew Forum on Religion and Public Life titled "Faith in Flux: Changes in Religious Affiliation in the U.S.," those who have left Catholicism outnumber those who have joined the Catholic Church by nearly a four-to-one margin. It is tempting to conclude that the church is dying.

What is more accurate, though, is that the church is changing in dramatic ways. What we should ask is, could this be a very good thing for us? Could it be that Christianity has a brighter future?

At the end of 2010, I attended a denominational conference featuring Diana Butler Bass as the keynote speaker. As she unpacked this moment in Christian history, she presented a helpful framework for understanding the paradigm shifts in which we are living currently. She referenced the work of William McLoughlin, professor of history at the University of Chicago, who published a small book in 1978 called *Revivals, Awakenings, and Reform*. McLoughlin highlighted five significant social transitions that have marked human history and suggested that we are living through a transitional moment in this cycle. He argues that we are experiencing a fourth "Great Awakening" that is having seismic effects on our institutions, collective beliefs, and behaviors. He writes:

> Great Awakenings (and the revivals that are part of them) are the results, not of depressions, wars, or epidemics, but of critical disjunctions in our self-understanding. They are not brief outbursts of mass emotionalism by one group or another but profound cultural transformations affecting all

Americans and extending over a generation or more. Awakenings begin in periods of cultural distortion and grave
personal stress, when we lose faith in the legitimacy of our
norms, the viability of our institutions, and the authority
of our leaders in church and state. They eventuate in basic
restructuring of our institutions and redefinitions of our
social goals.

The pattern usually expresses itself in this way:

1. *Crisis of Legitimacy:* Individuals lose their bearings;
   neurosis, psychosis, and violence increase in prison
   populations; family breakdown.

2. *Cultural Distortion:* People conclude their problems are
   not personal, but are the result of institutional dysfunction;
   the prevailing order has failed; ordinary techniques for
   handling social stress no longer work; no agreement on
   solutions; nativist/scapegoating movements develop at this
   point; these people resist change and seek to return to
   old ways.

3. *Appearance of New Vision:* Individuals appear who
   embody the cultural crisis and begin to articulate a new
   way of being, new insights, new understandings of identity,
   and new moral and ethical possibilities. Typically these
   people "shed new light" on ideals and practices that the
   community already values; they act as prophets of the new
   way that is faithful to what has gone before. They bridge
   old and new.

4. *Attraction:* Some people (often younger generations) begin
   to "get it" and begin to reorder their lives according to
   the new way of life articulated by the prophets; innovation
   and experimental stage, with both positive and negative
   consequences in the search for a new order. Revivals,
   conversions, and emotionalism are often marks of this
   stage as well. Conflict, division, and partisanship roil

between the followers of the new way and the maintainers of the old order.

5. *Transformation:* People who previously had been moderates or "undecided" regarding the necessity of change accept the new vision, new patterns, and new behaviors. Considerable revision of institutions, political reforms, reorganized communities, shifts in family structures, new economic practices.

Bass's conclusion was that we are living between cultural distortion and the appearance of new vision. It is important to note that these stages are not necessarily linear. You don't finish one and start another. They all are going on at the same time, with one having more control and influence than the others at a given point in time.

As I listened to her speak, I thought, "Yes, this makes sense to me." We are living through a major reorientation of Christianity. By reorientation, we do not mean to imply that we now have the chance to go back to the "golden age" of the Protestant church. No, today we have the chance to reorient Christianity in a way that may look less like the imperial religion of the state and more like the first-century church.

Neil Cole wrote a book in 2007 that helped me understand these shifts from a different perspective. In his book *Church 3.0*, he talks about the significant shifts in practice that we are seeing emerge in churches today. He references the process of developing software to illustrate how the church has changed during roughly the past two thousand years. Remember when Microsoft launched its first public operating system, Windows 95. Then came Windows 98, Windows ME, Windows 2000, Windows XP, Windows Vista, and today we have Windows 7. Each one of these represented a significant restructuring of the way computers processed and stored data. They were influenced by previous versions but were structurally different from them.

Between each of these new operating systems came a seemingly constant flow of smaller program updates. Every time we log onto the web, our computer checks to see if Microsoft has released a new update to fix issues discovered along the way, changing our systems from Windows 7 to Windows 7.1, 7.2, and so on. These are tweaks to the system, designed to make it more functional in its current environment.

Cole suggests that we as the church are living through a major system update. We began with Church 1.0 with the life and ministry of Jesus. Then we saw Church 1.1 emerge with the apostles and Church 1.2 with the journeys of Paul. The church experienced a major system redesign when Constantine sanctioned Christianity as the state religion, giving us Church 2.0.

Now Christianity is not a fringe movement but an imperial, institutionalized system of specially trained professional leaders, stained-glass buildings, and denominational structures. For the past fifteen hundred years, we have been living through Church 2.0 and its various updates. Today, we are in a different world. Church 3.0 is emerging in ways that are shaking the very foundation of the church, leaving it forever changed.

Church 3.0 is offering not only a new style of worship and organizational configuration, but also a new generation of imaginative leaders who are expanding the conversation about the future of the church. One of the exciting conversations in the United States is the emerging church movement. The emerging church movement overlaps a number of theological boundaries, creating conversations between evangelical, Protestant, Roman Catholic, post-evangelical, Anabaptist, Adventist, liberal, post-liberal, reformed, charismatic, neo-charismatic, post-charismatic, conservative, and post-conservative people. Many people prefer calling the movement a "conversation" to emphasize its developing and decentralized nature, its vast range of standpoints, and its commitment to sharing stories. What those involved in the conversation mostly agree on is their disillusionment with the organized and institutional church and their support for the deconstruction of modern Christian worship, modern evangelism, and the nature of modern Christian community.

	PAST?	FUTURE?
SEATING WHEN GATHERED	*Pews*	*Circle*
ENVIRONMENT	*Anonymous*	*Intimate*
LEADERSHIP SOURCE	*Higher Education*	*Multiple Paths to Ordination*
GROWTH	*Addition*	*Multiplication*
RESULTS	*An Audience is Attracted*	*Ministers are Mobilized*
MINISTRY PRACTITIONERS	*The Ordained*	*The Ordinary*
COST	*Expensive*	*Inexpensive*
MINISTRY SETTING	*The Meeting Place*	*The Market Place*
SUCCESS	*Full Seating Capacity*	*Full Sending Capacity*
CHURCH POSTURE	*Passive: "Y'all Come!"*	*Active: "We All Go!"*
ATTRACTION	*Felt-need Programming*	*Obvious Life Transition*
MODEL OF CHURCH	*Academy*	*Family*

Adapted from Neil Cole, *Church 3.0.*

In the United Kingdom, they are exploring their own version of renewal through "fresh expressions of church." The website *freshexpressions.org* describes it this way:

> Coined by the Church of England's report "Mission-shaped Church," the term has been used in the Church of England and the Methodist Church for the last five years. It is a way of describing the planting of new congregations or churches that are different in ethos and style from the church that planted them, because they are designed to reach a different group of people than those already attending the original church. . . . Fresh expressions are a response to "our changing culture." This movement assumes that the church is shaped by both the Gospel and the culture it is trying to reach. It is not meant to be conformed to culture; rather it

is meant to be appropriate for reaching and transforming a culture.

Fresh Expression churches often have unusual embodiments. There is a surfer church on Polzeath beach, a Eucharist for Goths in central Cambridge, a youth congregation based in a skate park, and a cell church among the Merseyside Police. Others are more familiar but in unfamiliar settings: church in a café, the function room of a pub, a school, a gym, or a sports club.

All of these expressions of church are ways of experimenting with what it means to be the Body of Christ. This is just one example of how the future of the church is going to look very different from past versions, and there are many reasons to celebrate this. While we always experience pain and loss as we transition through changes, the coming change in Christianity is its resurrection, not its death. Many lament the death of the church, but the church is not dying. In fact, we predict that the church is poised for explosive growth. After every significant historical shift in the church, we saw exponential growth in participation and conversions. As Phyllis Tickle notes in her book *The Great Emergence,* "One of the hallmarks of the church's semi-millennial rummage sales has always been that when each of these things is over and the dust had died down, Christianity would not only have readjusted itself, but it would have also grown and spread." Already we are seeing the "appearance of new visions" in the renewed interest in Christian mysticism and spirituality in movements like the emergent church. We have every reason to be hopeful about our future.

Our hope as progressive people is particularly strong because the shifts in the culture leave the progressive church more closely aligned with the values of young people who are playing a critical role in the reshaping of the church. A 2007 study by the Barna Group reported on its website in an article titled "A New Generation Expresses Its Skepticism and Frustration with Christianity" discovered that just 16 percent of sixteen to twenty-nine-year-olds have a favorable view of the church. So where is the good news in that? Well, this is why they don't like the church:

- 91 percent think it is antigay, and they are not.
- 87 percent say it is too judgmental.
- 85 percent say it is hypocritical.
- 78 percent say it is old-fashioned.
- 75 percent say it is too involved in conservative politics.
- 70 percent say it is insensitive to those who are different.
- 68 percent say it is boring.
- 64 percent say it is not accepting of people of other faiths.

This could be great news, if mainline churches could distinguish themselves as *not* most of those things, and if they could find ways to cease to be old-fashioned and boring. After decades of being told that our decline was the result of being too liberal, we now find ourselves not being liberal enough for the value system of the generation we must attract.

In the fast-paced world of iPads, Twitter, video conferencing, and Facebook, young people find themselves craving authentic spiritual communities where they are known by name and nurtured in their own exploration of faith and spirituality. The core values of these younger generations are in some ways antithetical to previous generations. Previous generations valued collective input, organized institutions, conformity, rules, membership, and order. Started by the traditionalist and baby boomer generations, mainline denominations reflect these values structurally. Younger generations, however, find these values incongruent with their life experience and personal goals. For Generation X and millennials, the values of diversity, pluralism, entrepreneurism, independence, creative chaos, suspicion of authority, and globalization shape the networks to which they belong and the causes about which they are passionate.

For younger generations, "organized religion" in its present form simply makes no sense in a pluralistic world and does not add value to the busy lives they are living. Instead, they are using their entrepreneurial creativity to experiment with expressions of faith they call "spiritual, but not religious," as they reimagine rituals, songs, prayers, and practices that nurture their souls. These new churches and faith communities are connecting with the deep yearning of an entire generation who abandoned church but long for God. The church can offer more than connections; it can offer community. In a world changing at the speed of the Internet, the church can offer transformation, and, in a world where people live with few margins, the church can offer a space of grace in which to find meaning and purpose.

It is as if the church is poised and open to a new kind of spiritual experience that moves people away from frantic patterns of modern hyper-productivity and toward a renewed sense of awe, mystery, and incarnational life. We want to feel God, to relish the Sacred, to ponder the questions of meaning, faith, and transcendence. Our hungry souls yearn to be fed in communities that transform us — moving us from meaningless doing to holistic being — and reconnect us with our life source and Savior.

If the church is hungry, what is giving us sustenance? Who are our nurturers and our prophets? Where are we seeing the appearance of new vision that restores meaning and order to our life experience? While no one can predict with certainty the shape and form of the church, we can identify the emerging cultural values that are influencing its formation:

- Religious and cultural pluralism

- Environmental concern

- Care for one another

- Incarnational faith

- Reclaiming of spiritual practices

- Compassionate capitalism

- Authentic, experiential worship

Religious and Cultural Pluralism

In seminary I took a course called "The Many Faces of God" taught by an Indian Hindu-Christian professor. On the first day of the course, he walked into the room, looked at us and said, "There are many paths to God. Yours is not better or worse than mine. We are all seekers on a spiritual quest." Then he held up a glass window with six panes and said, "Your eyes can only see God through this single bottom pane. You cannot see beyond your location, background, experiences, and education. My vision can only see through this top pane as a Hindu first and Christian later. By sharing our stories we can see more of God together than separately."

Pluralism is the idea that two or more religions with mutually exclusive truth claims are equally valid. Thanks in large part to globalization and technology, people now have the capacity to share life stories, perspectives, and wisdom in ways that often show we have far more in common with one another than differences. We are meeting people from far-off lands and learning of cultures of which we had never even dreamed. All of this has opened our minds to the possibility that we are all spiritual beings on a quest to find God and each of us holds a sacred truth.

Diana L. Eck at Harvard University has been studying the ways in which religious pluralism is changing the American religious landscape. In her essay "What Is Pluralism?" found at *pluralism.org*, she describes religious pluralism this way:

- First, pluralism is not diversity alone, but the *energetic engagement with diversity.* Diversity can and has meant the creation of religious ghettoes with little traffic between or among them. Today, religious diversity is a given, but pluralism is not a given; it is an achievement. Mere diversity without real encounter and relationship will yield increasing tensions in our societies.

- Second, pluralism is not just tolerance, but the *active seeking of understanding across lines of difference.*

Tolerance is a necessary public virtue, but it does not require Christians and Muslims, Hindus, Jews, and ardent secularists to know anything about one another. Tolerance is too thin a foundation for a world of religious difference and proximity. It does nothing to remove our ignorance of one another and leaves in place the stereotypes, the half-truths, the fears that underlie old patterns of division and violence. In the world in which we live today, our ignorance of one another will be increasingly costly.

- Third, pluralism is not relativism, but the *encounter of commitments*. The new paradigm of pluralism does not require us to leave our identities and our commitments behind, for pluralism is the encounter of commitments. It means holding our deepest differences, even our religious differences, not in isolation, but in relationship to one another.

- Fourth, pluralism is *based on dialogue*. The language of pluralism is that of dialogue and encounter, give and take, criticism and self-criticism. Dialogue means both speaking and listening, and that process reveals both common understandings and real differences. Dialogue does not mean everyone at the "table" will agree with one another. Pluralism involves the commitment to being at the table — with one's commitments.

Being "at the table" together is a core value of the progressive church and will become even more important as we transition into the future church. Churches of the future will value the contributions of other faith traditions as a way of opening another "pane" of insight into God. You will be as likely to hear a quote from the Bhagavad Gita as from the Bible and share in interfaith dialogue as a way of understanding your own faith more deeply. We are not talking about merging faith traditions, but an increasing acceptance and respect for the ways other faith stories help us to understand our own.

Of course, this is not a vision that everyone embraces. While progressives seek to move beyond mere tolerance, fear and fundamentalism have joined forces to resist this movement. The violence perpetrated and wars fought in the name of God may make religion repugnant to an entire generation if we do not assertively articulate another way. The apocalyptic imagery of fundamentalist Christians and Muslims should frighten us all. The progressive church must find its voice if religion is to be seen not as the mortal enemy of the human race.

While religious pluralism has been a value of the progressive church for some time, the strong emergence of cultural pluralism is reshaping the church as well. The United States is becoming one of the most culturally diverse countries in the world, and with that diversity comes an influx of new traditions, practices, languages, songs, values, and norms. Added to this is the powerful catalyst of technology, allowing us, through live webstreaming, to worship and converse online all across the country. Rev. Eric Elnes, a dynamic and creative thinker, and the leaders of Countryside Community Church UCC in Omaha, Nebraska, had the vision of creating a portal to a new Christian faith for the twenty-first century. They launched *onfaithonline.tv*, which hosts web programs that educate and inspire people seeking the unconditional love of God. They also created Darkwood Brew, an online and onsite coffee shop that they describe as "a groundbreaking experimental web television program and Christian worship service." Darkwood Brew is a new experiment in cultural pluralism, combining the historic and modern practices of faith to connect with a global audience.

As we move at light speed into these coming years, we predict that American culture will be changed forever by the meeting, merging and melding of many cultures. The church, in turn, will reflect those changes. With the rise of terrorist and fundamentalist sects in all major faith traditions, it is all the more important that we find the places, stories, and values that join us together so that we might embody the shalom — the peace that passes all understanding — that we all seek.

Environmental Concern

In 2006, former Vice-President Al Gore was featured in the documentary *An Inconvenient Truth*. Using interactive charts of the environmental effects of global warming, and sharing stories of people affected by climate change, the film showed that global warming was not just a political issue but is, in fact, the greatest moral challenge facing our generation. Viewed by more than 5 million people, it turned out to be the tipping point in global awareness of the environmental issues facing our planet. After the movie's release, thousands of nonprofit and for-profit organizations popped up across the world to raise awareness of climate change, as well as a host of other issues like conservation, renewable energy, air pollution, genetic engineering, slash-and-burn policies, mountaintop removal, urban sprawl, water pollution, and recycling.

Churches of all denominations are now part of this national movement, and the progressive church has claimed this as one of its most passionate commitments. Across the country, churches are "greening" their buildings and conducting energy audits to find ways to conserve. Churches like Circular Congregational Church in Charleston, South Carolina, have built eco-friendly buildings that include grass-topped roofs for water cooling throughout the building and use only eco-friendly building material in the construction of the new structure.

This trend in eco-awareness will continue as churches explore what it means to "do church" in more environmentally conscious ways. More and more churches will host meetings online so that members do not drive to the church. The churches that continue to use bulletins — which will be fewer and fewer — will have recycling bins in place after the service to collect them. New churches will continue to move away from the need to build their own buildings, opting instead for the "recycled" space of already constructed store fronts, bars, theaters, and sanctuary time borrowed from existing churches. Instead of building bigger buildings, churches will find ways to better utilize the space they have, both on their property and in their community. In their book *When Not to Build*, Ray Bowman and Eddie Hall point out that, on any given Sunday, every community has a stunning amount of unutilized community space in libraries, corporate conference rooms, coffee shops, restaurants, YMCA buildings, etc. These spaces are available for small group gatherings, meetings, Bible study, choir and band rehearsal — anything. That said, our recommendation is not to move your children's ministry offsite; parents like to be close to their kids. Everything else could be hosted offsite, saving your church money, expanding your capacity for ministry, and saving the environment!

Care for One Another

In a December 2010 *Time* magazine article titled "What Really Happened?" the editors looked back at the past ten years of American history. What they discovered was a series of national institutional failures that have left the world disoriented and shaken.

The writers started with the botched presidential election of 2000 where, for weeks, we debated hanging chads and who would be our next president: a failure of our political system. In 2001, we met terrorism face-to-face in our homeland on September 11: a failure of our national security. In 2002, we watched the start, and immediate missteps, of the war in Iraq, which enmeshed our country in a war without clear objectives: a failure of our military system. We also saw the impact of programmers who cracked the encryption codes on CDs and DVDs, creating the ability for everyday people to set up peer-to-peer file sharing, threatening the economic foundation of the entertainment industry: a failure of our mediating systems. By 2003, we saw the Chinese economy take off, rivaling the U.S. economic power for the first time in history: a failure of American economic superiority. In 2005, we were glued to our television sets as we watched in horror as Hurricane Katrina decimated thousands of homes and lives, and then we watched the U.S. government fail to respond to the disaster as levees broke, gangs took over the streets, and a city drowned: a failure of our physical and political infrastructure. By 2008, we were in the throes of the greatest economic collapse that the world has ever seen, threatening the middle class in the United States and leaving thousands of people homeless, unemployed, and poorly educated: a failure of the American economic system.

As the bumper sticker says, "If you aren't angry, then you aren't paying attention." While we in the church tend to think that institutional failure is just about us, the truth is that we are living in the midst of a much larger social shift that is destabilizing all of our critical institutions and creating a sense of fear, uncertainty and anxiety about our future.

In the midst of this change, the progressive church will rediscover its voice. The promise of the Gospel is that fear never has the last word, and that faith, love, and hope are always our paths forward. The future progressive church must reinvent itself in the midst of this global disorientation and step into the gap that today divides rich and poor, healthy and sick, educated and uneducated, legal resident and illegal resident, gay and straight, female and male. The church should be the place where these barriers are erased and genuine community forms to care for people victimized by the failure of the institutions built to support them. Reformed by a value of pluralism and diversity, the church provides a place for people to be known, loved, and supported as the world around us wrestles with disillusionment, violence, fear, and failure.

Albert Einstein, of all people, perhaps best articulated the role of the church in our emerging world when he said:

A human being is part of the whole called by us "universe," a part limited in time and space. We experience ourselves, our thoughts and feelings as something separate from the rest — a kind of optical delusion of consciousness. This delusion is a kind of prison for us, restricting us to our personal desires and to affection for a few persons nearest to us. Our task must be to free ourselves from the prison by widening our circle of compassion to embrace all living creatures and the whole of nature in its beauty. The true value of a human being is determined by the measure and the sense in which they have obtained liberation from the self. We shall require a substantially new manner of thinking if humanity is to survive.

The progressive church has a role to play in freeing us all from the prison of isolation and reconnecting us to one another and ourselves.

Incarnational Faith

By incarnational, we mean to invoke "embodied" or experiential faith. The progressive church of the future will be deeply experiential, connecting both the head and the heart to a daily experience with God. For too many years, mainline Protestant churches have fed the head with scholarly sermons, theological treatises, and an explosion of Christian books focused on theory, while neglecting the yearning of our hearts to experience the life-giving, transformational power of God. We have been on a major head-trip.

The church of the future will find a balance of sound theology and incarnational experience. Education is still highly valued, but the church must find ways for people to *feel* God through paintings, music, meditation, body prayer, sacred conversations, labyrinth walking, pilgrimages, yoga, serving meals to the poor. In other words, we will embody God within the world and, through that experience, find God within ourselves. Elizabeth O'Connor says it so well: "A person is in his/her own very being a gift....However...we do not experience ourselves as gifts until we are engaged in the act of creativity." The progressive church is, and will be, exploding with acts of creativity.

Today, many of our new churches are renting space from art galleries or hanging paintings by local artists on their walls.

Sculptures and painted glass sit on altars and are dotted around worship spaces as a way of connecting the sacred to the secular, divine art to human art. Churches like Neighbor's Abbey in Atlanta use art to draw the congregation into, according to their website, "generative conversation with each other and their neighbors. The outcome of these conversations includes new works of worship: worship gathering programs, original music, artwork, poetry, and community action." All of these expressions are designed to connect the body to the Spirit, deepening faith and transforming the soul.

Reclaiming of Spiritual Practices

Along the same lines of incarnational faith and authentic worship, the future progressive church is one based on helping people deepen their connection to God through spiritual practices that make the sacred experiential. In particular, emerging churches are reaching back to the ancient spiritual practices of the first-century church, which gave the church its passion and meaning, and then reinterpreting those practices in our culture. There is renewed interest in practices like labyrinth walking, Taizé chants, traveling on pilgrimages to ancient holy places, Lectio Divina, meditation, and new interpretations of the sacraments. As Marcus Borg says in his book *The Heart of Christianity,* "Practice is about living the Christian way."

In other words, Christianity is becoming once again a way of life, not just what we practice on Sunday. In their essay "Christian Practices and Congregational Education in Faith," found in *Changing Churches: The Local Church and the Structures of Change,* Dorothy Bass and Craig Dykstra write that Christian practices "are the things Christian people do together over time to address fundamental human needs, in response to and in the light of God's active presence for the life of the world." Many congregations, they go on to write, are becoming monastic communities with porous boundaries. They reconnect people with the corporate and individual faith practices that shape their personal narratives. Pastors increasingly are called abbots, and faith communities become places of spiritual retreat, connection, and respite. Above all, the spiritual practices that shape the church constitute parts of the larger human life and provide us ways of understanding them within a particular Christian narrative.

Recently prayer started making a comeback among the most popular spiritual practices. Thanks in large part to a meshing of the Eastern religious practices of yoga and meditation with the Western religious concept of prayer, more and more people are creating space in their days and homes for quiet time for meditation and reflection. Prayer is evolving from a childlike list of wishes that God might or might not grant, to a more intentional communing with a sacred part of us, which many would say is God. As Bishop John Shelby Spong says in an interview in the *Living the Questions* series of videos, prayer allows us to participate in the God process of expanding life and increasing love and enhancing being. Prayer is not something you do; prayer is something you are.

The reclamation of the ancient spiritual practices will reshape the practice of worship and the form and structure of church. Diana Butler Bass says it best in her book *The Practicing Congregation:* "In an age of fragmentation it may well be the case that the vocation of congregations is to turn tourists into pilgrims — those who no longer journey aimlessly, rather, those who journey in God and whose lives are mapped by the grace of Christian practices." The future church once again will be a place of transformational connection to the divine that brings new life and learning to those who journey within.

Compassionate Capitalism

The failure of the American banking and financial system in 2008 created a growing awareness that there is something truly sinister about profit-driven greed. We all watched as the government, using our tax dollars, bailed out dozens of banks deemed "too big to fail," while average Americans lost their jobs, investments, retirement accounts, and homes. While we are still reeling from the shock of losing so much of our hard-earned money and the stability that it brings, we now are awakening to a reality that there has to be a better way. Corporate greed destroys the soul of a nation, and consumerism is destroying the soul of everyday Americans.

The statistics on average individual debt have not been encouraging for many years now, but the recent financial crisis has made matters far worse. According to a recent article on *MSN.com* by Kim Khan called "How Does Your Debt Compare?":

- About 43 percent of American families spend more than they earn each year.

- Average households carry some $8,000 in credit card debt.

- Personal bankruptcies have doubled in the past decade.

Americans are drowning in debt. If the church is to have any significant impact in the lives of people in the future, we must begin addressing the epidemic of consumerism and economic injustice.

Many churches are offering money-management programs for members, but far more needs to be done. The obsessive consumption that has taken control of us is more deeply rooted in feelings of insecurity, fear, power, and control. While we know these things corrode our lives, we cannot seem to break free of the nonsensical illusion that more stuff brings more happiness. We fail to connect that we are trying to meet internal needs with external wants, and we move further and further away from the contentment that we all seek.

The church must find ways of waking people up from this life-taking slavery to stuff. It was not an accident that Jesus spoke about money more often than any other issue; it is the most dangerous seductress of the human heart, luring us away from our own wholeness.

Authentic, Experiential Worship

The great mythologist Joseph Campbell noted in his conversation with Bill Moyers in the book *The Power of Myth* that, in his experience, people actually were not seeking the answer to the meaning of their lives; they were seeking the experience of being alive. So it is with worship. The future progressive church understands that people are no longer seeking information *about* God or the Bible. They are seeking experiences *of* God both in community and in their daily life.

Authentic, experiential worship will be the hallmark of growing, vital churches in the future. Worship must be authentic in the sense that the rituals, readings, stories, and theology speak in honest, meaningful ways to the human/divine relationship. The style of worship will not matter — organs, bands, hymns, praise songs — all of that is secondary to the deep longing to come into the presence of the Holy One and, if only for a moment, be transformed.

That said, the quality of the worship experience is paramount. In the age of multimillion dollar television productions and Broadway shows, bad music and poor preaching have no place in church. Worship must make people laugh and cry and leave them changed so that they might go into the world with the sure knowledge that they are children of God, loved now and forever.

◆ ◆ ◆

It would be bold, even arrogant, of us to suggest that this is an exhaustive list of the characteristics of the future church. Even as we write this, we thought of many other characteristics we want to include. What we do suggest is that, while the form of church is changing, the function of the church is not. The progressive church of the future is still in the business of transforming lives. How we do that is changing — thanks be to God — but the core of who we are as a body always will remain the same. We are expectant with possibilities, ready to give formation to a mystery we do not yet understand in a world we only barely know. What we can know for sure, though, is that our future is unlimited.

T W O

Where Do You Want to Go?

In the book *Alice in Wonderland,* there is a wonderful scene between Alice and the Cheshire Cat in which Alice asks for directions:

> ALICE: Would you tell me, please, which way I ought to go from here?

> THE CAT: That depends a good deal on where you want to get to.

> ALICE: I don't much care where.

> THE CAT: Then it doesn't much matter which way you go.

> ALICE: . . . so long as I get somewhere.

> THE CAT: Oh, you're sure to do that, if only you walk long enough.

Like Alice wandering aimlessly through Wonderland, too many of our churches wander through their lives not knowing which way to turn. Richard Hamm, in his book *Recreating the Church,* writes:

> If the eight mainline churches are not lost, they have certainly at least been wandering since 1968; wandering and wondering what happened. "Why don't the things we used to do work anymore?" "Why are we declining in numbers of members and in resources?" "Whose fault is it?" "Has God forsaken us?"

28

The only way out of this wandering wonderland is to acknowledge where we are and decide where we want to go. As the Cheshire Cat wisely reminds us, we will surely get somewhere if we walk long enough.

The Bell Curve

Just as you and I experience birth, growth, decline, and death, so do the organizations we create. At each stage of our life, our perceptions, goals, needs, and challenges change as we adapt to the changes in our world and develop greater capacities within ourselves. These changes — both personally and organizationally — can be diagramed effectively on a standard bell curve:

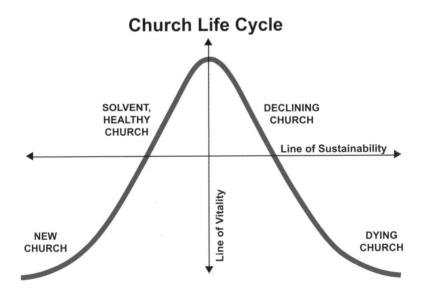

Every organization experiences growth and decline. These stages are marked by certain milestones that point to changes in organizational health and development. To better understand this, we use two lines of reference drawn in the shape of a cross through the middle of the curve. A vertical "Line of Viability" represents either the numeric growth on the left side of the line or the decline of the church on the right side of the line. The horizontal "Line of Sustainability" represents the financial health of the church, with those ministries below the line being dependent on denominational funding (or funding beyond the giving levels of active participants) and those above the line being sustained primarily through participant giving.

These lines divide the church life cycle into four quadrants: new, growth, decline, and dying. Each of these quadrants represents very different stages and requires different leadership skills, resources, ministries, strategies, and possibilities. The table on the following page explains some of these distinctions.

Understanding where your church is on this life cycle is the starting place for diagnosing your condition. Are you a Quad I, II, III, or IV church? What leadership challenges are you facing? What skills must you learn to navigate through these phases?

The Key Indicators

Here is another way to think about this. Congregations have four indicators to measure health: energy, inclusion, programs, and administration. At each stage in the life of a church, these indicators play a more or less active role. These roles are indicated by the upper and lower case letters on the graph.

The "Energy" indicator highlights the level at which the congregation is motivated into action around the vision and mission of the church. It speaks to the spirit of the faith community as well as its passion about its ministries. The "Inclusion" indicator highlights the dedication and enthusiasm of church participants to invite people to be a part of the ministries of the church. It speaks to an outward focus on growth and an intentional commitment to hospitality. The "Program" indicator highlights the level at which the church is able to start, grow, and maintain ministries that transform both the community and the people within the church. These are particular to each church context and to the needs of the people within the church. The final indicator, "Administration," highlights the need of every church to

Quads	Characteristics	Issues/Challenges
Quad I	Driven by vision with a strong emphasis on growing the fellowship through outreach and evangelism.	Making the vision generational and sustainable over time.
		Developing theologies around evangelism and growth.
	Passionate about their mission and values and excited to share those with friends and networks.	Balancing giving ministry and receiving ministry.
		Encouraging fluid leadership styles from pastor and leadership teams for growth.
		Pastoral leadership shifts.
Quad II	Driven by program development and staffing opportunities.	Funding existing ministries at higher levels.
	High energy programs, administration, and inclusion.	Buildings, parking lots, programs.
	Positive spirit, low anxiety, high functioning system.	Inward and outward focus on ministry and inclusion.
	Strong sense of mission, purpose, and vision.	
Quad III	Relationships, programs, and management are dominant.	Because vision is no longer driving the agenda, management takes a greater control.
	Vision is no longer dominant.	
	Passive rather than active.	Morale tends to waiver in selected portions of the congregation.
	Successful in many areas but lacking a clear focus.	Strong need for re-visioning and/or strategic planning.
	No felt need for change.	
Quad IV	Decline of ministries, programs, and staff.	Because of decline and reduction of ministries, dealing with feelings of nostalgia, disappointment, and anger.
	Hope that tomorrow will bring the return of yesterday.	
	Strong emphasis on commitment from existing members.	High conflict between leaders and staff.
	Blames others for holding them back.	Often the congregation will have low self-esteem and issues of failure.
	Stress on pastoral leadership.	Asset allocation: What to do with assets and buildings if they close.

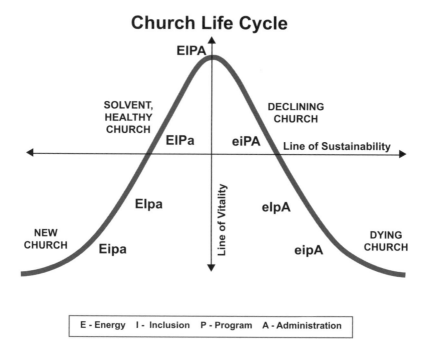

Church Life Cycle

have systems that promote growth through policies, procedures, and staffing. Collectively, these indicators tell a story of where a church might be in their life cycle. Let's look at each phase more closely.

Quad I: Birth and Childhood

You can't help but notice the joy and excitement in the eyes of new parents as they talk about the moment when they first saw their new child. They start by counting the fingers and toes and then take countless pictures so that they can remember the moment and share it with others. The birthing experience changes them and becomes the formative narrative for their collective lives as a family.

So it is with new churches. The birth of a new church is a joyous and exciting adventure marked in a number of ways depending on who is telling the story. Some new churches look back on their birthing moment as the time when a small group of people sat in someone's living room and dreamed of starting a new faith community in their neighborhood. Others mark their birth as the day when their doors opened for the very first time and they hosted their first worship service. Still others talk about their birth as the moment the pastor knocked on their door and said, "I have this crazy idea about starting a new church. Want to help?" All of these stories, and these birth experiences, profoundly shape the ways churches develop in succeeding years. Our birth narratives are deeply formative in who we become later in life.

Most new churches are "birthed" over a period of six months to two years, starting with planning, praying, and preparing. In these early days, the leadership of the new church focuses on the vision, mission, and purpose of this new faith community. In most cases, a small group of people develop a collective dream of what this new church will look like and how it will impact the world. Then they set out, often with baby steps, to make this dream a reality. They have planning meetings in people's homes and meet in restaurants or coffee shops to talk about what needs to be done. They begin thinking about ministries, programs, meeting spaces, worship experiences, spiritual formation, and invitation. The energy and passion for the church come primarily from the pastor and the launch team members. At this point, the indicators of inclusion, programs, and administration are all low because the group remains relatively small.

The driving questions during the birth of a new church have to do with vision and mission. The new church has to answer:

1. Who are we (individually and as a collective group)?

2. What needs in our community are we seeking to meet?

3. What values do we honor and allow to shape us?

4. How would this community be positively changed through our presence?

Many churches start with a generic vision of being a friendly, welcoming place for people to come and experience God. The trouble is that all churches should be friendly and welcoming. New churches that grow to be older churches have to find their *unique* voice, vision, and mission beyond the normal "we are nice people" mantra. They need to know why they exist now, in this particular moment, and what change they are seeking to bring to the world. They must understand not just why their church *could* exist, but why it *should* exist. If a new church skips over this step in the attempt to rush to be a "grownup" church, its future will be compromised. In fact, the most common mistake that new church leaders make is launching too soon without having done the important vision and mission work at the beginning.

As the church moves from birth to childhood and more people become involved, the primary energy of the church expands beyond the leadership team to a wider group, and *inclusion* becomes a value of the community. Inviting people to this growing "movement" becomes a high priority, and the growth of small groups helps keep people connected and building relationships.

During this phase, the size of the "grownup" church becomes more visible. If the new church can develop effective systems for multiplying small groups, the chances are strong that, over time, the church will become a program or corporate-sized church. If the groups become "ingrown" or closed, and starting new groups is a constant challenge, the chances are strong that the church will remain a family or pastoral-sized church. As the saying goes, "What you do today is who you become tomorrow."

As churches grow, they experience brief moments of growth and moments of plateau. Usually around the second year, as a new church moves from infancy to childhood, it experiences a brief plateau as people adjust to the new growth of people and ministries. At this point, we usually get panicked calls from the church planters wanting to know what they are doing wrong. Everything was going so well, and then, suddenly, they stopped growing. In most cases, this is normal and the growth soon resumes. What happened? They encountered the "Step-Fix Theory."

As organizations grow, they go through periods of rapid growth and high excitement. As more and more people join ministries, the programmatic and administrative structures of the church have to catch up. We have named this the "Step-Fix Theory": you take one step up and then pause to regain your balance, footing, and bearings.

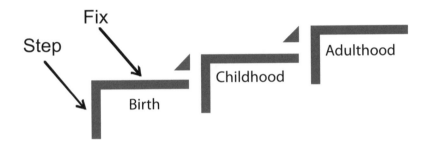

The church starts with an exciting launch and the growth of small groups. This is represented by the vertical line of the step. In order to support this growth and prepare for greater growth, the church has to build some internal structures like financial, communication, and administrative systems. Let us emphasize that these systems are designed to promote greater growth in ministry, not greater control *over* ministry. As the church begins developing these systems, the energy of the leadership temporarily shifts from an outward focus (invitation and growth) to an inward focus (structure and capacity).With the new systems in place, the focus realigns toward outward growth and the church moves to the next level.

In the Protestant church, the Step-Fix Theory moves in a general pattern during the first few years. In year one, the church typically grows to around forty active participants. The second year often brings the most exciting growth period when the new church grows to about sixty active participants. With that transition comes new structural needs that require a revision of the systems that supported the church to that point. The third year a new church will grow from sixty people to seventy people while it builds the internal structures needed for growth. In the fourth year of a new church, we typically see another growth increase to around eighty to a hundred people. If the new church successfully redevelops its supporting structures, the growth will continue in the following years.

In the typical church model of the 1950s, a church passes the line of sustainability when it reaches around 150 people and has achieved "critical mass" — enough people to support its ministries. Today that number changes based on the model adopted by the church. House churches and those with bi-vocational staff use different measurements of sustainability given their differences in overhead costs. Emergent church models have lower ministry costs and different measurements for sustainability. The relevant question is where is the line of sustainability for your church?

Quad II: Adulthood

Once a church has achieved critical mass — enough people to financially sustain its existence without denominational funding or grants — the church moves into the second major phase of life. The church begins focusing on developing dynamic ministries and programs that affect change in the community and support the needs of those participating. The energy level of the congregation is still high as is the passion for inviting people to be part of the church. Now the church needs more developed and diverse programming to take it to the next level.

The church begins focusing on issues like staffing and structure to support the growing ministry demands. The early years of adulthood in churches are often like the early years of adulthood in human life: the pre-frontal lobes of our brains are not fully developed. We don't make the best decisions, and we think we know everything.

During these years, churches sometimes experience significant conflict for the first time. New people have changed the original vision, and new resources have created new possibilities. In more developed organizations, an administrative structure exists to handle these discussions. In a young adult church, this conflict both raises the awareness of a need for these systems and prompts a revisiting of the vision and values that shaped the church at birth. George Bullard explains this reality in many mainline churches in "The Life Cycle and Stages of Congregational Development":

> Two visions of the church seem to be dominant in the congregation. People who affiliated with the congregation during birth hold one vision. This is a vision of a strong worshiping community with intimate fellowship and care, and meaningful, corporate spirituality. People who are affiliated with the congregation during adolescence hold another vision. The programs, ministries, and activities of the congregation that met specific needs of the family or household attracted them. Their vision is one of a full-service, family-focused congregation with opportunities for meaningful, individual spirituality.

In most cases, the tension that arises provides an opportunity for refocusing on the collective vision and a chance to recommit to the value of moving forward together. As churches move through this phase, there are some critical questions that must be addressed with regards to:

- Staffing
- Management systems
- Programming needs
- Spiritual formation needs and community connections
- Member assimilation
- Buildings and physical space needs
- Conflicts and competing priorities

As those needs and questions are addressed, all key indicators in the church begin functioning in a healthy productive rhythm. Energy, Inclusion, Programs, and Administration work together to make the church a transformative experience for the people and the community. It is church at its best!

Quad III: The Declining Church

Something happens. It is subtle at first. Something shifts. People get tired. Programs become predictable. Giving stagnates. People start complaining. Energy drops. As a church begins a turn into decline, you almost always can measure it by a clear drop in the congregation's energy for ministry. Fundamentally it has to do with an internalized complacency and separation from the passion and vision that first created the church.

If the church continues to proceed without any intervening revitalization efforts, the first things to decline are the energy and impulse toward inclusion that brought such health and vitality to the congregation at earlier points in its life. People are either consciously or unconsciously becoming aware that something is off about their congregation. Some may be able to name the disconnect; others simply will have a gut feeling. Either way, they stop inviting their friends, and those who visit often get the sense that there's simply something odd in the energy of the place.

Astute leaders will catch this early and start working on renewal before the church drops below the line of sustainability. In their book *Holy Conversations,* Alice Mann and Gil Rendle offer a great example of the redevelopment loop with their graph of the "Life Cycle of a Congregation." They present three models for turning a church away from decline: ongoing renewal, revitalization, and redevelopment. The sooner the leaders of a church react to the decline, the more likely they are to successfully renew the church.

Ongoing renewal can be as basic as reconnecting the congregation to their vision, mission, and values through, for example,

Life Cycle of a Congregation

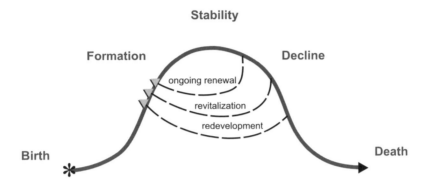

small group activities, sermons, congregational dialogues. Many churches have mastered the art of featuring narratives or testimonies in their services. Each Sunday they invite different people to talk about why the church is valuable and meaningful in their lives as a way of reminding people why the church exists. Sometimes they record the person talking to ensure control over the quality and quantity of the story, but, every time, the stories are powerful, touching, and memorable. They reconnect the wider community with why their church matters and how they are making a difference in people's lives. Renewal is simple reconnecting with your original calling, contemporizing it to your present environment, and living it out through your ministries.

Sometimes, however, ongoing renewal is not enough. When churches internalize dysfunction or unhealthy systemic behavior preventing it from growing, the more directive work of revitalization is needed. Revitalization forces tough questions about the identity of the church, the values of the church, and the call of God on that church. It often involves stopping ministries that no longer work and starting new ministries that do. Budgets that have served the church well for years need to be reimagined, reflecting the changes in the church. The leadership examines every area of the church, looking for ways to bring new life before they find themselves in the valley of dry bones.

Quad IV: Old Age and Death

When a congregation has been declining for some time, losing people, money, programs, and energy, redevelopment is the last option. It often is very costly. By now, the church has dropped below the line of sustainability and is living off of endowments or investments. In a near panic, facing the reality of their possible death, the congregation initiates a campaign to invite people to their church. Instead of inviting them to vital healthy ministries, however, they are inviting them to a depressed community that is struggling to pay bills and keep their doors open. The sense of grief is often overwhelming, and a desperate attempt to maintain the programs that defined the church in its golden years often can create church fights of magnificent proportions. Administration often becomes the primary focus of church leaders as they struggle to balance budgets, fill slots on committees, and maintain systems that no longer have impact or influence. These are devastating years in the life of a church where well-intentioned people do all they can to maintain a church that has lost its vision. As we all know, "Where the vision has perished, so do the people."

The final stage of the church life is often portrayed by a small group of aging people administering the final days. At this point, they have given up hope for revitalization, and they preside over the closing of their community of faith. Walking with a church through this stage of their life is a sacred and devastating experience — and one that is not inevitable.

Is It Really This Straightforward?

In a word, no. Church life really doesn't fit into the nice simple bell curve that travels along a predictable path. Churches are living organisms with all of the quirks and oddities one would expect from a human organization. Our experience in working with hundreds of churches is that the life cycle looks more like a report from the New York Stock Exchange than a simple curve, though the curve is helpful for framing the long-term shifts.

The truth is that churches go back and forth between growth and decline, sometimes within the same week! We often can chart upticks in growth with the arrival of a new pastor or the launch of a new program, and then we watch it decline when conflict arises or ministries become stale. Whereas the bell curve suggests that as the church goes through renewal it "goes back" to what it once was in its better days, the reality is that it becomes something almost entirely new. Renewal is not about "going back"; instead, it is about remaking the church into what God is calling it to be and do today.

We are not suggesting that death is inevitable for any congregation. The life cycle of the church is not determined by any set number of years and theoretically can go on endlessly. Death comes only to those churches that lose their passion for life.

The purpose of this book is to help you understand your church and, if it is not what you want it to be, equip you to change it. We are convinced that the progressive church has a bright future. You are a key to making that future a reality. Take a look in the mirror. Where is your church on this life cycle? What key indicators are driving your ministries? What changes do you need to make to turn your church toward growth?

An Alternative Future: Planting Vegetable Gardens

If death is not our only future, how do we change those churches that are deeply steeped in decline and despair? How do we renew old, dying churches housed in old, rotting buildings?

We plant vegetables in our flower gardens.

Let me say that again: We want to suggest that for you to claim the best possible future for your congregation, you may have to plant a vegetable garden in your flower bed. Many of our churches are in pretty buildings with great stained glass and oak pews. Nicely dressed, well-behaved, properly mannered people attend our churches. We do worship decently and in order, following ancient liturgies and singing melodic music. They are flower gardens: things of beauty with a limited life expectancy.

Flower gardens are valuable, and the beauty they offer the world is appreciated. However, we live in a world of spiritually starving people and they can't, or won't, eat flowers. They want vegetables.

My suggestion is not that you root up the flower garden, but that you plant a vegetable garden in the same patch. You probably will need to keep the two gardens separate for a while because vegetable gardens tend to get messy. They have vines and things that run everywhere, and your peppers may just make your tomatoes spicy.

The future of the progressive church will rest in our ability to plant vegetable gardens. We are planting new churches all over the country, and that is a good thing. However, I think we also ought to plant new congregations within our old ones.

We have discovered that giving birth is easier than raising the dead — easier but a whole lot messier. Think about your last visit to a funeral home. It is neat, clean, quiet, and orderly. There are always flowers, never vegetables. Birth, on the other hand, is frantic, full of surprises, messy, and noisy.

We can either give birth to new congregations in our old churches or resign ourselves to being glorified funeral homes. Our best advice is to plant a vegetable patch of liberal, active, passionate adults who might just believe that the church of Jesus Christ can change the world.

THREE

AdMinistryation

To manage is to control. To lead is to liberate.
— *Harrison Owen*

In declining churches it seems that a small group of leaders carries a large load and always feels on the verge of burnout or exhaustion. In my experience, burnout is almost always the result of not doing the right things or not doing things right. A church that decides to be born anew may need to resolve to suspend many of the things they are doing and narrow their focus to only those things that are important to Jesus. In other words, they may do worship, small groups (community), and service, and nothing more. The toughest choice is limiting management and expanding ministry.

When starting a new church, the most dangerous mistake we can make is trying to act older and bigger than we truly are. "Acting your age" ensures that you avoid overpromising and underdelivering on the ministries that your new church begins. The temptation for church planters and new church leaders is to start committees rather than ministries — after all, that is what we did when we belonged to "grownup" churches. In a new church, however, the life, vitality, and impact come from the outward focus of the vision and mission, not the inward focus of management.

Permission-Giving Churches

We have coined a new way to spell administration as a reminder that the sole reason it exists is to facilitate and support the ministry of the church. Management, structure, and governance should never become an end, but must remain a means to an end. The church is the Body of Christ, and, to continue that allegory, administration is the circulation, support, and immune system that keep the body functioning. When it becomes visible and obvious, something is wrong. When it calls attention to itself and drains resources from the body, something is broken.

Management, governance, and administration taken together are the one thing that even dying churches seem to do well. Many have bylaws with more pages than the number of members still attending worship. It is clearly where their energy has gone and, probably, largely is still going. One wonders who or what they are trying to control. On the other hand, new, young, and thriving congregations often are guided by the principle "If no one is going to die, then give it a try." Their willingness to remain agile, responsive, and unregulated does get them into trouble at times. However, rarely are the challenges they face fatal, while overregulated congregations inevitably are being strangled by their own efforts to control everything. Jesus described the Spirit as being like the wind: beyond our control. Too often the declining church's response has been to nail all of the windows tightly shut to keep the wind out.

Becoming a permission-giving church may require the death of a whole herd of sacred cows. Being unwilling to make that choice, though, will lead to all those cows dying of starvation. This imagery comes from Bill Easum's book *Sacred Cows Make Gourmet Burgers,* in which he talks about the deadly dangers of churches addicted to control. He notes that "the Body of Christ is most effective when individuals are given permission to live out their God-given spiritual gifts on behalf of the Body rather than someone restraining what they can or cannot do." Easum goes on to list some of the forms that control takes in dying congregations:

- ◆ Our insistence on controlling what happens in our congregation and denominations
- ◆ Our desire to coordinate everything that happens or know about everything before it happens

- Our need to vote on everything, particularly everything new

- A parlor that few people use

- A kitchen that no one but those who are designated can use

- Money that is controlled only by the trustees

- An official body that has to approve every decision

Easum contrasts typical churches with what he calls "permission-giving churches." These churches live to say "Yes" rather than "No." Their mission is making disciples, not making decisions. They are led by people who do not need to artificially be made to feel important or empowered.

Permission-giving churches are possible only when we are permission-giving leaders. As we discussed earlier, the structure and empowered leadership of church are changing in radical and exciting ways. One of the most significant changes is in the role of clergy. For the past fifteen hundred years, the church has been led by an elite, specially trained group of scholars and pastors who have served as preachers and teachers. The cultural expectation was that these specially trained clergy would serve as resident "experts" in matters of the sacred. Lay people came to church to learn from their pastor how to lead better Christian lives. To be a pastor was to be a full-time shepherd, preacher, and teacher with a special status both in the church and in the community.

Today, however, churches are turning more and more to bi-vocational pastors or strong lay leaders, largely because they are declining and no longer able to pay for full-time clergy to serve them. New churches led by passionate clergy and lay people who are seeking ways to "talk with" people instead of "talking at" people are emerging across the country. Sermons or, more specifically, brief meditations, now are followed by "talk back" opportunities where people in the pews can respond to ideas or thoughts they heard in the sermon. Doug Pagitt describes this shift well in his book *Church in the Inventive Age,* when he says, "The ability to preach and teach is taking a back seat to the pastor's capacity to create and facilitate open-source faith experiences for the people of the church." Church is now about experiencing the Divine in organic, expressive, creative, incarnational ways. Permission-giving is not just an ideal; it is a core value of the future church.

Permission-giving churches must have a clear vision of where they are going and identify core values that guide who they are and who they are becoming along the way. Decisions must be congruent with the guiding principles, and, therefore, they almost always can be made by those doing ministry rather than a committee managing ministry. For these reasons, permission-giving churches tend to have teams rather than committees. These teams come together to accomplish something, not to decide something. The team ceases to exist once the goal is met. Imagine that: a group that does something rather than decides something and doesn't always feel a need to meet or even to exist.

Permission-giving churches, rather than voting to make decisions, seek to discern what is needed and where the Spirit is leading and then strategize about how to get there. The team is made up of those who feel called to the task at hand rather than those who are elected or appointed by some power source. A team comes into existence when two or more are called to a ministry that is congruent with the vision and values of the church. "If no one will die, give it a try." People come together out of a sense of common passion rather than being made to feel guilty or needing to feel artificially important. It is true servant leadership: those who serve lead.

In permission-giving churches, the VIPs are those who do ministry, not those who give or withhold permission. No one may even know the identity of the governing board, but everyone knows the real heroes. They are the ones who help make ministry happen. Those who do the ministry make the decisions affecting the ministry. If money is needed, they often identify sources of funding, one of which may be the church's treasury. When that is true, they make their case to the authorizing body just as they would to any granting agency. Everyone is clear, though, what is being sought is money, not permission. Unless the ministry violates the mission or the values of the body, only Jesus has the authority to withhold permission.

In 2008, Rev. Susie Smith and twelve lay leaders started Peace Congregational Church, UCC, in Clemson, South Carolina with the vision of becoming a community of hope that proclaims God's extravagant welcome, embodies the radical love of Jesus, honors the interconnectedness of our lives with creation, and empowers all people to grow toward wholeness. Susie wisely understood that people today are craving an experience of God, of the Holy, and they come to church seeking that transformation. They do not come because they want, or need, more meetings in their lives.

During a visit to Peace Church, I watched Susie meet the new people and connect them with others in the room. I laughed as one participant explained, "When Susie walks toward you, you know that you are about to be put to work changing the world." Susie asks two questions:

1. What are you most passionate about in this world?

2. How can we as a faith community help you live into that passion?

The heroes of Peace Congregational Church are the people doing the ministry, proclaiming God's radical welcome, embodying the radical love of Jesus, and empowering others to grow toward wholeness. Susie and her leadership team simply help the Spirit to move through the church by opening the windows of creativity, permission, and appreciation.

Transitioning from a controlling church to a permission-giving church is difficult. Not surprisingly, it often results in generational conflicts. Those who have managed the affairs of the church probably are much older and have grown up in a culture with many more rules. They are comfortable and, in fact, more secure when they know all the boundaries and have all the answers ahead of time. Younger people have grown up with almost all the information in the world available to them. They are quite accustomed to "Googling" to find any information they need. They also have lived and worked in a world where the speed of change has made almost everything a living lab. Any job, project, or program is an experiment that might or might not work, and if it takes very long to decide, organize, and implement it, it isn't relevant because the situation has changed already.

These two opposing realities are not imagined. The generation in control must decide how many more fifty-somethings are being born. If their own generation is not the future of the church, they must relinquish their need for control and begin to trust. The church *is* a faith-based organization after all. Mistakes will be made. Programs and projects will fail. The wisdom of two athletes must guide us in this regard:

> I missed more than nine thousand shots, which means I failed over and over, and *that* is why I succeed.
> — Michael Jordan

> I missed *every* shot I didn't take.
> — Wayne Gretzky

Permission-giving churches must give ministries permission to fail. That is why they often are started as a sort of lab. A small group of people with limited investment try out a program or project as an experiment in learning. With that approach in mind, failure is actually success because you discovered what doesn't work. In this approach, having older people involved with young people may help encourage patience. All too often, if something doesn't provide immediate results or gratification, the plug is pulled, when a bit of time or patience might have given the yeast time to rise or the seed time to sprout. Those who actually have baked bread and planted gardens seem to understand this principle and are critical partners.

In actuality, the transition from controlling to permission-giving is challenging for those in places of power and control, but in the end it is often a relief and an experience of renewal. They have waited longingly for their declining church to do more. When new and younger people suddenly are given permission to try, the energy and accomplishments breathe new life into those who simply have held it all together for so long.

When Bud Precise, a retired United Methodist pastor, came out of retirement to become the pastor of Pilgrim Church, UCC, in Birmingham, Alabama, he looked out at the congregation of thirty-five aging people that first Sunday morning and knew that they were in for an interesting journey. They wanted to renew the church, and Bud understood that the best way to do that would be to empower younger voices in the congregation. He started by asking his son and his son's friends to take the lead. They began attending worship more consistently and serving on committees. They spoke out about the issues that concerned their generation and encouraged the church to advertise themselves as the "liberal" church in town. (I did mention that we are talking about Birmingham, Alabama, right?)

New people began noticing the church, and the number of first-time visitors increased. They sold their building, recognizing that it was taking too much of their focus and energy away from ministry to maintain it, and they rented space in a downtown Baptist church. As an entire congregation, they made the choice to reinvent themselves, calling on the younger voices among them to lead the way. While many of the older congregants still serve in key leadership positions, everyone recognizes that their future is in being the liberal church in the city, which means making room for everyone, young and old.

Pilgrim's story is still unfolding. They recently called a younger woman to be their pastor, and they are reinventing themselves once again as new people join the church. Their future is bright, primarily because they are living into the values they claim: to be a community of integrity bringing justice and peace to the Birmingham area and the larger world.

Permission-Giving Leaders

The truth is that the conversion to permission-giving must begin with the pastor, who is often more entrenched in the existing systems than anyone else. While there is probably no awareness of this, they will be the ones most disturbed when they find people doing ministry they have never even seen in the name of the church. It is most irksome for the pastor to hear secondhand that their church is involved in something they have never heard about, let alone started or approved. If they don't know about it then they don't get credit for it. The existing system of control requires the pastor to be the one always pushing the church to do more, always pleading the case on behalf of new people wanting to start ministries. Losing this role is most disconcerting because it disturbs a careful homeostasis that has been worked out for years.

Strong and healthy pastors will have all these feelings, fears, and resistance, but they will know their source and resist the urge to act on them. Learning to be the chief cheerleader and mentor for the leadership of others is a new role for most pastors, but it is one that empowers the church more than their willingness to work seventy hours a week. This may mean that the pastor must take responsibility for encouraging something that does not have official approval. "Well, let's start slowly and see how it works. If it takes off, we may need to take it to the council to get their blessing."

In churches that succeed in making this transition, the elected body — board, council, vestry, consistory — finds that they end up being responsible for the things in the church that should be most important to them: finances, property, and legal policies and obligations. They may even have time to be involved in some of the other ministries that intrigue them.

Even permission-giving churches need to have accountability and boundaries. The role of leadership is still to establish, clarify, communicate, and refine the vision, mission, and values of the church. The world is changing at such a rapid rate that these pillars must be examined and reframed frequently to be effective. Leadership is also responsible for calling ministries into alignment. Their role is to create an environment in which teams of disciples of Jesus are able to appropriately live out their call. Permission-giving never means allowing anything to go on in the church that violates moral or legal standards; it means giving people permission to live like Jesus with compassion and grace.

De-Net Your Church

The root of ad*minist*ration must be ministry. Most mainline churches older than two decades need to appoint teams of de-netters. The image is that the church is designed to be a great eagle — powerful in flight, great in vision, not generating the wind, but knowing how to spread her wings and soar on the currents of the Spirit. The trouble is that that kind of freedom — and, I believe, that kind of power — terrifies most Protestants. Thus we began to tether the church to the earth, lest it take off in a direction we did not anticipate or perhaps could not control. Today, this great eagle that was meant for the skies is so entangled by a net of constitutions, bylaws, policies, boards, and committees that the wind would have to blow mightily to even ruffle the great eagle's feathers.

The *only* additional task force most churches need is a team formed once every five years, and for one year only, called "The Liberating Team." It should be made up of the kinds of members the church is seeking to attract and with a limited number of "powerbrokers," though a couple of "influencers" would be good. Their task is to examine ruthlessly the systems and structures that guide and govern the church and make recommendations to the congregation for changes that will liberate the church and better empower it for ministry. They are called to clip the cords of the net that holds the church back from responding to the Spirit's call. Ultimately, their goal should be to recommend the elimination of anything that:

- Isn't congruent with the vision and values of Jesus, since the church is the resurrected Body of Christ.

- Discourages new ministries from being attempted and people from answering what they believe is God's call on their lives.

- Doesn't empower decision-making by the smallest number of people at the level closest to where the ministry is being done.

- Doesn't protect the church from real legal or moral liability. Care must be taken to ensure the church is protected, but also that fear doesn't become the governing principle for administration.

- Doesn't make sense to new members, young people, entrepreneurial souls.

Welcome Our Guests to a Safe Home

The one area of regulation that needs regular re-examination and likely should be strengthened in most churches is the "Safe Church" policy. The recent epidemic of sexual abuse scandals has heightened anxiety, but few churches have put policies into place that will protect people from abuse and the church from the subsequent liability. Ignorance will not be a legal defense for any church, but we are now guilty of neglect for knowing but not putting proper policies and procedures into place.

Of even greater concern should be our failure to protect our children properly. Have you ever walked through your building looking through the eyes of someone who might want to abduct a child, for example, like an estranged parent realizing that this is the one time he or she is able to access the child because the other parent or guardian is at worship. Old buildings with many entrances are particularly vulnerable. A child running to a parent they haven't seen raises no suspicion at all, but could be kidnapping nonetheless, and now your church is an accomplice. Do all your children's workers have background checks? If not, you may be guilty of negligent hiring.

Every denomination has resources for Safe Church policies. Ironically, this is the one area of control and management where many mainline churches have been negligent. What does it say about your church if it has a policy about who can use the church parlor or kitchen, but not about who can pick up a child from Sunday school? What it says is that those who write the policies (and probably give the money) use the parlor, but not children's Sunday school.

While a discussion of Safe Church policies may seem odd in a book about church planting and congregational revitalization, neglecting this can kill any hope for a healthy congregational life. A scandal certainly can kill a church. However, what may be just as deadly for the church's future is failing to make parents feel that their children are absolutely safe when they are in our care. Parents who grew up in our church will look at our children's ministry through the eyes of their own warm and loving experience. However, new people, particularly people with limited experience of church and churches, will be jaded by all the news reports, and they will expect that the church should be just as secure as the school or daycare where they drop off their children. In some settings, this may even mean the visible presence of a security guard or off-duty police officer on Sunday mornings. The safety of their children is something about which this generation of parents has much more anxiety and awareness. Giving new parents a copy of your church's Safe Church policy on their first visit lets them know you were prepared for them and their child. It also can be a great evangelism tool. Imagine a mother telling her friends who also are mothers how seriously you take keeping her child safe and secure when the child is in your care. It is a great witness to what the church *really* values (much better than that sign in the parlor or kitchen with all those rules).

We Live in an Age of Technology — Use It!

These days ministry uses a variety of tools that didn't exist twenty or thirty years ago. The web has become our most effective tool for introducing people to our churches. In fact, you would be wise to think of your church website as your "front door." The overwhelming majority of those who visit your church will check it out online first. Have you looked at your website lately through the eyes of first-time visitors? Is it warm and inviting? Is the information they need obvious and accessible? Does it reflect who your church was, is, or hopes to become? Can they communicate with you through it? Are you capturing their information?

A few words about website design: technology is rapidly changing our lives — the way we communicate, shop, find information, spend our free time, plan our vacations, find that "special someone," etc. The church should be ahead of that curve and using technology to its fullest extent. Sadly, it seems we are always twenty years behind the rest of the world. During the past five years, core design and functions of websites have shifted from online brochures to interactive experiences that build ongoing relationships. With platforms like Joomla, Dropal, WordPress, Wild Apricot, and others, websites now provide a way for you to build a relationship with the people who visit your site.

For example, when people visit your homepage, they might be greeted by simple questions, such as, "Are you interested in learning more about our church?" When they click on that button, they are directed to a set of pages on your site with information specifically targeted to answering their general questions and connecting them with volunteers or staff who can reach out to them. You also might ask, "Are you an active participant in the church?" If they click on that, they will be directed to more "insider" information about small group meet-ups, upcoming events, or prayer requests. The key is using your website to *connect* people, not simply relay information. If your website does not engage people and require that they *do* something in response, you should consider redesigning your site. Remember: this is the new front door of your church. It should usher visitors in and welcome them to the family.

It would be very helpful to think for a moment in terms of modern businesses. Today nothing is more important to a contemporary and growing business than to capture as much information as possible about potential customers. There is a strong principle here that has been sorely neglected by the church.

When Robert Schuller was the senior pastor of Garden Grove Community Church, he decided that he wanted to build a building that would capture the imagination of people and leverage his message and ministry into global prominence. He did that and was, at one point, the best-known American non-entertainer in the world (though some might argue he actually was an entertainer). His services were broadcast around the world from a building that soon drew almost as many visitors as Disneyland.

When Schuller first approached Philip Johnson, known as the "dean of American architecture," about building his Crystal Cathedral, Johnson was dubious. First, Schuller arrived at Johnson's New York office unannounced. He told the receptionist that he was there to "talk about a job." When that message was relayed, Johnson told her to tell Schuller that they had no openings at the moment, but, if he would leave his résumé, they would get back to him. After that rocky start, Schuller then had to convince Johnson that, yes, he really did want to build a glass cathedral-sized church in an earthquake zone. Ever ready for a new challenge, Johnson was most concerned about where the money would come from for a project on a scale such as this. This was in 1975, but even then Schuller knew a secret that most churches have yet to learn. He told Johnson that he would raise $18 million with a mailing list. And he did.

Schuller understood then that getting, retaining, and managing contact information was critical. That is even truer today. Churches that want to grow must structure themselves in such a way that their database (also known as Customer Relationship Manager, or CRM) is their most valued asset. If the building catches fire, leave the hymnals and the offering but take the database. Actually, the database should be so valuable to your church that there is no need to take it because it is backed up offsite or maintained "in the cloud," so there is little risk that it will ever be damaged or lost.

If you are starting a new church, this advice is invaluable. Your job is to network! You must meet as many people as possible in your community and invite them to be part of helping you change the world. When pastoring a new church, I would make a point every day to meet with at least ten new people who had no previous connection to the church. I would meet them in coffee shops, community events, the soccer field — everywhere and anywhere. In the course of the conversation, I would get their contact information. On the back of their cards, I would make notes about what I learned about them from my conversation. Our leadership team of ten other people was doing the same. Then we would take all of the contact info (usually in the form of business cards) and put them into a database.

Every Monday morning, I would print out a report with all of the people listed for that week, including where they lived, their passions, talents, previous church history, family connections, occupation — everything that might trigger a connection with someone already in our church community. We then would pull together the leadership team and start playing matchmaker. We would assign these new people to our small group leaders based upon our best guess of affinities. Those leaders would call or email the new people and invite them to a small group gathering, coffee, or whatever felt right for that person. When we started using our contact management system — paying attention to who was in it, why they were in it, and how we could strengthen our relationships with those people — our retention rate skyrocketed!

Remember this: the vast majority of people who come to church for the first time come through the personal invitation of someone else. If you invest your time in training your people to invite and use your contact management system to feed them names, you will save a great deal of money in advertising costs.

There are numerous church databases available at low cost. However, it is important to look at this as an investment for the future, an investment that will build the church of the future. A few years ago a database would have been little more than a place to store names and addresses. Today, though, the database has become the core of the engine that runs the church. It should be able to integrate with giving, stewardship, and fundraising (Note: these are three separate things) as well as the accounting system. At the end of the month, a well-integrated data system will prove that the money taken in and the money that went out balances perfectly. While not as critical to new people as the safety of their children, un-churched people need more assurances that their money is being adequately and accurately cared for. The days of the church books being kept in the trunk of the treasurer's car have passed. New donors want financial information in a form that says you value their money as much as they do.

An effective database also needs to keep all the information possible about members. There is no reason the church shouldn't send birthday and anniversary greetings to every member of the church. It all can be automated, but you, of course, have to get members' birth dates and you have to have a system that will manage that information. It is increasingly critical that the database interact with the church's website so that you can ask members to enter that kind of information on the website and, thus, directly into the database. It is also important that the system allows for pastoral notes. As a church grows, it is impossible for the pastor to recall the exact date on which a parishioners' parents or partner died, but the database can retain that knowledge and remind you so a note can be sent. It is also important that there is a place to put confidential notes. If there was a problem with a person being abusive or inappropriate with children and you failed to make a record of it, you have great liability for future problems, even if you have moved on to another parish.

The database is the key to communication, which we will talk more about in the chapter on marketing. Once upon a time, medium and large churches had staff positions that managed evangelism. Today a database can automate much of how the church responds to, connects with, and stays connected to visitors. Well-managed data can enable a team of lay people to do what a full-time staff person might once have done. This is true of pastoral care as well. A team of comfort ministers might send handwritten notes to people on the anniversary of a death.

As important as the computer system is, of equal importance is how you get information or perhaps just the fact that you do. Getting full and accurate information from those who attend regularly is not so difficult. Many databases have places to put a person's picture, which is especially easy if the church has a pictorial directory, and, in fact, most systems can pull people's profile pictures and basic contact information from their Facebook accounts.

Imagine how helpful it is if you are asking a lay person to visit someone who is sick and you include a picture of the person in the email. So often they will say, "Oh yeah, I know her; I just didn't recognize the name." You also will be able to say, "And her birthday is next week, so you might wish her an early happy birthday." In a church with hundreds of members, the pastor, staff, and leaders can get a weekly list of birthdays, and, when they see the people on Sunday, wish them a happy birthday. In a world that is increasingly depersonalized, this can make a big impact and make people feel genuinely valued and included. It doesn't require you to have a great memory; the computer has it for you. All you have to do is read the list and remember it in an hour or so when you see the persons. Again, having pictures can really help. With digital photography, it is easy enough to find volunteers to take photos of everyone. Certainly every new member should be photographed, and, as nice as posting the photos on a bulletin board is, putting them in your database

will have a much more lasting impact on the church's ability to
serve the new members.

We hope we have made the case for how important having an integrated database is to your growth or renewal as a
church. Choosing a system can be overwhelming, especially since
technology changes so fast. To help you in your discernment,
here are some key features of a strong CRM that every church
should have:

* Easy member information management

* Integration with your church website, online giving system,
  social networking, mail and accounting systems

* Donor management

* Varying levels of permission

* Resource management (organize small groups, ministries,
  and volunteers)

* The ability to mail-merge letters

* Email

* The ability to create and manage specific queries

* Reporting

* Web-based user interface with off-site data storage.

There are many systems available at varying cost points. The best
strategy is to assess your needs and determine how you want to
use the system. Then compare your needs with the functionality
and price of the various systems available. You also can find
helpful comparison studies of competitive systems online.

Connecting with Visitors

If we are asked one question more than any others in working
with new and renewing churches, it is "What is the best way to
get contact information from visitors?" The answer is simple. In
our experience, pew pads are still the best.

Americans fear public speaking more than they fear dying. When churches ask visitors to stand so that they "might be recognized" or raise their hand so that an usher can bring them a "special visitor card," what they actually are doing is making people feel isolated, singled out, and vulnerable to a group of people they do not know. Singling out a person who finally has found the courage to visit a new church is extremely counterproductive and it can cause them to be so uncomfortable that nothing could persuade them to return. Many churches have cards in the pews that they ask visitors to put in the plate rather than an offering. "Today you are our guest, so there is no expectation that you will give us money. What we do ask you, though, is to give us information about how we can contact you. The pastor would like to write to you and thank you for coming, and we'd like to send you a gift from the church to show you how honored we are that you worshiped with us today."

Two critical points here: first, ask them to give you the information; second, tell them exactly what you are going to do with it. The "gift" can be something simple. It could be a CD of the church's favorite songs, or a DVD with information about the church and perhaps a recording of a famous artist or speaker who has visited the church. Be creative. It can be cheap, but not tacky. How you respond to first-time visitors is your second chance to make a good first impression. Done badly, it will be your last.

More visitors will give you their information if you ask them to do something that *everyone* in the room is doing. For example, when you pass registration pads down the pews, ask everyone to register, including the first-time visitors. This system ensures that they are not singled out as new or different. It also allows you to track members' attendance and be alerted after someone has missed two or three Sundays. Following up before they have been gone longer than that will discourage drift and attrition. It also says, "Your presence is important to us, and your absence is noted." Given the mobile nature of many urban congregations, weekly registration allows people to help keep your database up to date. The post office may tell you if someone moves. However, unless you ask, no one will tell you their new email address, and 90 percent of our communication soon will be done electronically.

Remember: this is about adMINISTRYation. It is about collecting and managing personal information in such a way that the church is better able to minister to its members and to the community. Target marketing is possible if we do this well. Imagine having an author come to speak at your church. This person may attract people who never would have attended otherwise. What a great thing to know who was there, and then, if during Lent you decide to study another one of that author's books, you can target those who heard the author speak and invite them to the study. There are unlimited ways to effectively use information, but only if we collect it and manage it well. The computer can be our best tool for growing our churches and making people feel more included and cared for. It also can generate a lot of work. That sounds scary to leaders who already are feeling overworked, but there are also lots of opportunities to empower people to genuinely be in ministry:

- Pick up coffee and donuts and ask a group of retired folks to come down Monday morning to go through the registration pads. They can input the data and pull lists of visitors and those who have missed three weeks.

- They can email the list to other teams who send handwritten notes. Maybe one of your shut-ins has beautiful handwriting, so the Monday morning folks may drop off the list to her along with preprinted and stamped envelopes.

- If people put prayer requests on the registration pads, volunteers can send the prayer list to the prayer team, who might also send notes to those for whom the church is praying.

• "Missed" you emails are good, but a handwritten note from the church telling people they were missed is powerful.

Pastors need to write notes all the time, but they should be the kinds of notes that can come only from them. All other notes should come from the real ministers of the church: the members.

Building Better Budgets

I was recently on a sailing trip with four other couples. At the start of the trip, one of the women immediately went to the front of the boat and sat down to enjoy the ride. When her husband asked where she was going, she called back and said, "I want to see where I am going, not where I have been."

Church budgets tend to have a backward view. Many churches are using outdated financial structures and templates that no longer reflect the ministry of the church they have become. They are a long list of line items with numeric figures next to them that fail to communicate any compelling story of vision or mission. How many of us have been to congregational meetings where the leaders in the church stand up, show a spreadsheet with hundreds of tiny numbers, and then ask us to write a check? That is not the most inspiring way to build or present a budget.

The budget should reflect the mission of your church, and it should be one of the most inspiring documents that you produce all year. Here is a test to discern if you have a problem in this area. If the leadership knows how much the church's utility bill is this month but doesn't know how much your church is spending on youth ministry, that should be a red flag that priorities are out of alignment.

When creating a church budget, ask your team this question: "What kind of church do we want to be five years from now?" Then set your team on a path of discerning what that might look like for your financial structure. We are fans of narrative budgets for the simple reason that they force you to connect your financial strategies to your missional strategies. Narrative budgets allow you to tell the story of how your church is making, and will make, a difference in ways that are accessible to people who are not good at reading spreadsheets.

Ever year in one church, we did a sermon series called "Why We Love This Place." Usually this was a five-to-seven-week series where we would feature key ministries of the church. We would tell stories (in the South we call them testimonies) where people would talk about the difference the church had made in their lives during the past year. We would remind our participants of why the church existed, for whom the church existed, and how we were doing in living up to our mission. These worship services became the greatest pep rallies we would ever need to revitalize our church each year.

We did them because we wanted to feel good about ourselves. We intentionally scheduled this series right before we started the budgeting process for the following year because we wanted every person focused on the ministry rather than management. When we started our budgeting meetings, we wanted them to see faces instead of numbers, lives instead of bottom lines. We wanted them to designate their money to making a difference, not maintaining an institution.

Our tendency as church leaders is to engage administration from points of extreme: either too little attention to the value efficient administration brings or too much emphasis on the management of ministry. However, remember this: when people walk through your doors, they are not looking for ways to fill their time; they are looking for ways to transform their lives. They do not need more meetings in their week; they need more of God in their days. They come to you with their hopes, brokenness, fears, passions, and talents and they are looking for companionship on their spiritual journey, for grace, acceptance, and help in becoming the people God is longing for them to be. They come to you looking for ministry, not management.

FOUR

The Church of Facebook

Back in the good ol' days we would have called this secret of church renewal "evangelism." Of course, in the progressive church, that has become a four-letter word. The reasons for that are as many as the examples of abuse we all could cite. Still, as proponents of taking back words, we suggest that perhaps the progressive church should reclaim the word "evangelism." In fact, perhaps God is calling every one of us to become "liberal evangelists." People are looking for what we have found:

- Grace, forgiveness, mercy, reconciliation
- Community, connections, friends, relationships
- Meaning, purpose, mission, calling
- Hope, joy, God!

To withhold these gifts is as unconscionable as knowing a source of free and abundant bread, but refusing to tell the hungry. People are seeking a liberating word, and we have it. Liberal evangelism is simply having the courage to speak that word and offer that bread. We never would force bread on the gluten intolerant, but neither should we withhold the water of life from the parched and thirsty.

We who are people of faith believe that we have found a great gift; why wouldn't we share it? Our hesitancy, hyper-sense of propriety, and reticence have left most modern Americans with the impression that, if they want to be Christians, their only option is to turn to a church that is sexist, homophobic, nationalistic, pro-war, and right-wing.

Your church probably does not have those characteristics, but how would they know? Church marketing is nothing more, and nothing less, than proclaiming, in clear and creative ways, the good news that we have come to know. We are prone to use secular language to talk about spiritual realities. In part, that is because spiritual platitudes give religion a bad name. The other reason, though, is to get us religious types to think about ancient subjects in new ways. So if secular or business language bothers you, every time you read the word "marketing" pretend it is Greek for evangelism.

So what are the seven secrets of effective church marketing?

Marketing Begins at Home

First mobilize the congregation. Your congregation is your witness. This is both good and bad news. Consistently, every survey says that the number one reason people choose a church is that someone invites them. This is good news for new churches because people are excited about this new adventure, there are no historical conflicts, they probably like the pastor or they wouldn't be coming, and, best of all, they have lots of friends who do not go to your church or probably any church.

This principle is bad news for long-established churches. Your congregation is your church's reputation. If there has been a conflict, the community wants no part of it. Rebranding a church that has a bad reputation in the community almost requires the death of the old church and the birth of something new. Few churches actually have any idea what the community thinks of them. For better or worse, in most cases, they don't think of them one way or the other.

In her book *The Turnaround Church*, Mary Louise Gifford writes that, when she arrived in Wollaston, Massachusetts, many of the people in that community thought the church was closed. In other settings people believe the church has been turned into a school or a daycare facility since that is the only activity they see happening on the campus.

We have discovered that one of the best ways to find out what people really think about your church is simply to ask them. When we work with new churches or churches in renewal, we start by literally walking the streets and talking to the people who live there. We ask them questions like:

- Why do you love living in this community?
- What kind of social and political organizations do you belong to?
- What concerns do you have for your community?
- Do you think this neighborhood would embrace a new church?
- Do you currently attend church? Which one? What do you like about that church?
- What kind of church would you be interested in attending if you don't attend a church now?
- If we were to plant a progressive church in this neighborhood, would you come?
- Do you have any friends that would also be interested in being part of a faith community?
- Who else should I talk to? Can you give me their contact information and/or introduce me to them?

You will be amazed at the helpful information you gather by talking to the people on the streets, the servers in restaurants, the shopowners, the school officials, and the public servants. In many ways, what you learn in these conversations will be more valuable than all of your online demographic research.

In long-established churches, the fact that marketing starts with the congregation could be bad news because most of your congregation's friends probably are already in the congregation. That is why new people are your best hope for future growth. They are positive and energetic. They want to share their new home with others, and they have many more friends outside the church than inside. That is why the best hope any church looking for renewal has is when it finally attracts a critical mass of new people to begin to shift the culture toward the future rather than the past.

Whether yours is a new or renewing situation, you must mobilize the members of your congregation in the inviting process. Even if they do not end up inviting anyone personally, they need to be prepared to welcome them authentically and be their host.

The other way that marketing begins at home is that your building or campus is your biggest billboard. For new churches, this goes to the issue of site selection: is it accessible, visible, attractive, appropriate for who you are trying to attract? For renewing churches the campus often speaks volumes about the true state of the church, or perhaps about what it is the church really values. In denominations like the United Church of Christ, many churches are made up of people from good German stock, so the buildings are in pristine condition. The pews may be empty, but they are clean and polished.

The trouble is that many mainline churches are also impregnable. These churches seem to take Luther's "mighty fortress" imagery literally. We call churches like this "Fort God." You can't find your way in to save your life, and there are no greeters outside or signs to offer you a clue that you deserve to get in anyway.

We need to see our meeting space through the eyes of reluctant first-time visitors, who aren't at all sure this is the right place for them. Is it obvious that they are welcome, expected, and appreciated? Is our church a warm hospitable place for them and their children, or is it an impressive historical institution to which they must seek admittance and be judged worthy? What does your building say to those who have a painful history with the church?

Consistent Persistence Is Vital

An example from old media is insightful here. On the radio, by the time a song is climbing the Billboard Charts, radio DJs are sick of it. Marketers generally say that a person needs to hear your message seven or eight times before it begins to penetrate. Direct mail experts will tell you that if you plan to do fewer than four mailings you are wasting your money, because the mailing doesn't start to pay for itself until after the fourth or fifth mailing. If you get a response rate of half of one percent on the first mailing that is considered a great success. That is a parable about every other kind of marketing, advertising, or evangelism. In the storm of noise and imagery, repetition is necessary even if our marketing is very well done.

Just remember: by the time your message finally penetrates your congregation, you will be sick of it; by the time it penetrates your community, your congregation will be sick of it. Those commercials you once thought were clever, but now you are so tired of, are just beginning to succeed. You are probably only just now remembering what they are advertising rather than the commercial itself.

The other side of this secret is that your message, image, and branding must be consistent. Every time you change looks you have to start all over. That is why companies protect their logos so fiercely. They have spent billions of dollars branding that image on your brain so that just a hint of it brings the company to your mind. They did this by repetition and consistency.

Churches need contemporary logos, colors and images — a brand that communicates effectively to those you are trying to reach. Branding who you are called to be rather than who you always have been is much more difficult than you may think. It is critical that the existing leadership understand the purpose of creating a new image that they will be resistant to because it actually won't appeal to them. It shouldn't. Your brand should appeal to the congregation you are hoping to attract.

The website *www.breakthroughchurch.com* says this about church branding:

All too often we lean toward safe, bland, me-too branding. This is understandable, but it is also not a good idea, that is, if we want to be even moderately effective. Churches can easily find themselves safe...and invisible...to just those people you really want to reach.

To become viral or talked about...to be remarked about ...you have to become remarkable! Create a brand identity that...

1. ...is arresting, surprising, one that will get talked about.

2. ...unique among contending appeals.

3. ...has strong appeal to unchurched and dechurched people in the area.

4. ...you can adopt and live out in a remarkable way.

5. ...provides a long term, strategic fit in your city reaching goals.

6. ...provides many creative, adaptive, thematic spinoffs.

A church brand must be incarnational. It must be lived out in every area of the church and by every member and ministry of the church. For example, the brand of your church should show up periodically on members' Facebook pages. Perhaps for Easter they can replace their profile picture with your logo or an image of the church. Your impact can be multiplied exponentially with a brand that everyone embraces and is willing to use to represent them from time to time.

Stories

As Swedish filmmaker Ingmar Bergman said, "Facts go straight to the head. Stories go straight to the heart." In his book *Branding Faith,* Phil Cooke suggests that we in the church have "lost our story." He goes on to talk about how "every great civilization has creation stories and tales of great exploits that define their moral universe." That is true for us, of course, but, unfortunately, others are now telling our stories better than we.

In her innovative book *Dreaming of Eden: American Religion and Politics in a Wired World,* Susan Thistlethwaite develops "public theology" using the images and stories in our "Internet-driven culture" as the "stuff" of theology. She contends that our religion is rooted in the deep stories we tell, which we now tell in cyberspace. In *Dreaming of Eden,* she exposes the conservative-driven temptation to "escape to innocence" and shows progressives how they can develop and "use emotionally-laden, wisdom images that can 'go viral' because of the multiplication effect of the digital age."

Specifically, Thistlethwaite talks about James Cameron's movie *Avatar,* in which true life is centered on the Tree of Souls in the middle of the garden. In vivid 3–D, Cameron reminds us that our first and prime directive was to care for the garden that in turn cares for us. He tells our story powerfully, and, though we lack his $237 million budget, we, too, must find creative, passionate, and innovative ways to tell the stories of our faith and of our church.

Millions of people are telling the stories of their life on websites like Twitter and Facebook. They use pictures, links, music, and videos to personalize their own corner of cyberspace. Young people are remarkably and sometimes frighteningly self-disclosing. You can know more about perfect strangers than you do about your own children, or you can find out more about your own children than you really want to know with a simple visit to their page. The church must learn to tell its stories in these settings in a way that connects to the stories of others. We must be part of their story, and we must find ways to show that they are part of ours.

Again, people will not connect with information or theology or doctrine, but they will get hooked by the stories we tell. This is especially powerful if they can see themselves in that story, or if the way we tell our stories evokes memories of their own. In a lecture entitled "Preaching as Storytelling," Fred Craddock suggested that when people hear something we never said we are doing a good job because we are evoking from within them their own stories and connecting it to The Story.

In the Gospels, Jesus rarely preached, but he told stories constantly. Effective marketing uses every means at your disposal to tell your story and to tell The Story. Jesus seemed to understand that the fourth secret of effective communication is:

One Size Fits Some

Never has it been more critical that communicators abandon the "one size fits all" approach. Even Jesus used a variety of means to communicate his message. He understood that people take in information in different ways. For example, he sometimes used visuals:

- "Show me a coin. Whose image is on it?"

- "He took a child and placed him in their midst."

- "Look at my hands and my feet."

Jesus used visual images to communicate, often telling stories with such detail that, even two thousand years later, we can picture exactly what he is talking about. Of course, we all take in information visually, but some of us are more visually oriented than others. That is to say, some of us take information in visually first. Some of us are auditory, and some of us are emotive.

Do you know what you are? Do you know what your audience is? The first question is critical because, if we are not self-aware, we may not recognize that we are overly dependent on one form of communication.

Using colors, images, and shapes tells our story to certain people. For many churches, video screens have become the modern stained glass that serves to tell the stories of faith to those who learn best visually. The trouble is that preachers tend to be auditory, and, therefore, we may be trying to build a contemporary ministry with stale images and colors because we don't personally value and understand those images and colors. Every worship planning team should have a visual person, as should every evangelism/marketing team.

The principal means by which the church has communicated is the spoken word. Sitting through the announcement portion of most services will convince you that the leader believes the congregation is incapable of reading. Sermons remain the cornerstone of most Protestant worship, and it is most often a verbally didactic experience.

The American education system seems to believe that most people are auditory, yet, even for those who are, creativity and variation are vital pieces of comprehension. We all have heard a song and had the music transport us to a former time and place in our lives. Sounds have great power, and it doesn't always need to be the sound of the spoken word.

Is there a piece of music that communicates who your congregation is? Why not use a snippet of it when someone visits your website? Embed it in an email you send inviting people to your anniversary service, or play it through the sound system as people are gathering on Sunday mornings.

What is the feeling that you want to evoke? Anticipation? Hope? Devotion? Advertisers craft effective commercials that are emotionally evocative, appealing to those among us who are emotive. Coke, for example, understood from the very start that they weren't selling just flavored carbonated sugar water. Their image of Santa has come to be the standard by which all other Santas are judged authentic. Of course, Santa has nothing to do with soft drinks, but an effective marketing strategy anchored the two in the American psyche. Who would have thought that Clydesdale horses could be an effective sales tool for beer? Budweiser created emotional resonance using this breed so that every time you see one of those horses you think of their brand, and you feel a bit at least of the emotion they want to portray. Following the tragic events of September 11, 2001, Budweiser produced a commercial that was so powerful that they showed it only once. (The commercial can be viewed on YouTube: *http://video.yahoo.com/watch/62700/1705563.*) This is why effective storytelling is so important. Finding creative ways to tell our story, to tell The Story, and to let people tell their own stories is how we are able to move people. Moving people is a major key to transforming people's understanding of God and of your church. When was the last time something you did touched people? Well, that was too long ago.

Use All Your Tools

For the most part, our churches are communicating in the same way we did half a century ago. Oh, we may have a website, but most of the time it is essentially a static electronic version of the Yellow Pages ad. Few mainline Protestant churches actually are using their web presence as much more than a church sign on the Internet highway where people are zipping by at 4G speed.

If you wish to build a church of sixty-year-olds then advertising on the religion page of the newspaper and sending out a monthly printed newsletter is the way to ensure that no young people will ever know that you exist. However, if we are building a church of the future, and a church that has a future, we need to at least learn how to use the communication tools of the present and, hopefully, begin anticipating what opportunities the future offers.

Websites, email, blogs, Facebook, network marketing, Twitter, live streaming, YouTube, Flickr, and texting — our churches should be using all of these. There are a dozen other technologies that we should anticipate using in the future. Wouldn't it be great to actually be ahead of the curve for once?

Time magazine named Mark Zuckerberg, the co-founder of Facebook, its 2010 Person of the Year. In February 2004, Zuckerberg started the online social networking site that added its 550 millionth member just six years later. As *Time* magazine reporter Lev Grossman notes:

One out of every dozen people on the planet has a Facebook account. They speak 75 languages and collectively lavish more than 700 billion minutes last year on Facebook every month. Last month the site accounted for 1 out of 4 American page views. Its membership is currently growing by 700,000 people a day.

Where others looked at the Internet and saw a network of computers, Zuckerberg saw a network of people.

If there is one clear message for churches to understand it is that social networking is not a trend; it is here to stay. As Clara Shih writes in her book *The Facebook Era:*

> We are moving from technology-centric applications to people-centric-applications. We are improving the World Wide Web of information with a World Wide Web of people and relationships. . . . It is the end of the anonymous Web, and it is already transforming the way we work, learn, and interact across every aspect of our lives.

If the church is in the business of transforming lives, it would be smart to use Facebook as the conduit for beginning that work. The chances are good that a majority of your members and visitors have Facebook accounts. They most likely spend, on average, one hour per day browsing profiles of friends, colleagues, and organizations. They voluntarily have posted personal information about themselves on their profile pages that helps you know more about their lives, their passions, and those they love. They update their "status" with insightful information about their daily lives that could impact your pastoral care. If you are not using this platform to connect with your people, you are missing a huge opportunity.

Here is one way to understand the significant shift social networking can make in your local church. While many churches maintain (often poorly) individual databases, combining the database with a site like Facebook means you have more holistic, accurate, accessible information on the people in your church.

	Customer relationship management (CRM)/Database (One-Way Social Networking)	Social Networking Site
How are connections established?	You can buy lists of people who live in your area, ask members to give you information for their friends, or wait for people to walk through your doors.	Either party can initiate a connection, but the decision to connect must be mutual.
Where is the contact information displayed?	It is displayed in the account and contact record of a specific program owned by the church.	Social network profiles are the new CRM contact records.
Who are date, updates, and alerts shared with?	The church leadership receives updates.	Updates are shared with friends and networks, but users can adjust privacy settings.
What communication mechanisms are used?	You can use email templates, notifications, and alerts.	People communicate via Facebook messages, Wall posts, and notes.
Who updates the data?	The church administrator, volunteer, or pastor.	Data is updated from the bottom up; everyone is responsible for updating their own information.

Adapted from Clara Shih's Table 4.1 "Comparison of CRM and Modern Social Networking Site."

You may be wondering how on earth you are going to find the time to learn what all of these tools are, let alone how to use them effectively. Well, that really is the point of this secret. Our job as pastors and leaders is not to be the church, or to do the work of the church. Our job, at least according to the Bible, is to equip the saints to be the Body of Christ (Eph. 4:12). There are people out there who know a great deal more about all of this than we ever will. It is past time that the church asked them to help. If we do not mobilize those people to serve the Realm of God, then we certainly have not used all the tools God has provided. This is a great opportunity to engage young people and invite them to help give your church a greater virtual presence. (You don't have to tell them that they are the new evangelism team!)

Having said that, though, there are great sources of information that church leaders need to tap into if we are to be literate in this area. You may not feel like it is your responsibility to know about all of this. While we do not have to be experts in modern communication technology, to be illiterate about this is a foolish as insisting on writing sermons with a quill and ink rather than a computer. Leaders need to know enough about technology to at least know what is possible so that they can challenge the imagination of those who can make it a reality.

Think Multilevel

When I teach leadership development, I try to remind people that, while it is often easier to do it yourself, when you do that you spend time. When you recruit, train, and mentor someone else, you invest your time. With marketing, we need to begin to think of it as an investment. In most churches marketing consists of creating throwaway pieces given to their members.

Everything we create should be designed as though it is going to be forwarded and ultimately seen, heard, and felt by people who may not know our story. Email newsletters should be designed so members can forward them as invitations to their friends. Tweets should be written so people will re-tweet them. This, of course, means purging all communication of insider language and superficial piety. Oh, and never, EVER, use an acronym.

Progressive churches value inclusion. We have worked hard to make our music, and even the scripture, more welcoming. Ironically, mainline churches are the absolute worst about using "insider language." We must look at everything the church produces through the eyes of people who do not know us. We must listen to everything we say or sing through the ears of those who have been excluded by the church. We must evaluate the feelings we evoke through the hearts of those who have been deeply wounded by the church. If all our communication is reconsidered from those perspectives, we will find it more effective with those who are "insiders," but who don't feel nearly as included as we think. Again, every communication should be crafted with those who do not know you or your story in mind. Do not worry that the "insiders" will be offended or turned off. As the old hymn says, "I love to tell the story, for those who know it best, seem hungering and thirsting to hear it like the rest."

In the age of electronic communication, we all should know better than to put something in an email that we don't want the whole world to read. Well, the opposite can be true, as well. Craft everything as though you are welcoming new friends into the family and want them to understand fully who you are and what your church is about.

The church must learn to "think viral." Ralph F. Wilson wrote an early article about viral marketing and graciously granted permission for it to be reprinted here.

SIX SIMPLE PRINCIPLES OF VIRAL MARKETING
by Ralph F. Wilson

I admit it. The term "viral marketing" is offensive. Call yourself a Viral Marketer and people will take two steps back. I would. "Do they have a vaccine for that yet?" you wonder. A sinister thing, the simple virus is fraught with doom. Not quite dead yet not fully alive, it exists in that nether genre somewhere between disaster movies and horror flicks.

But you have to admire the virus. He has a way of living in secrecy until he is so numerous that he wins by sheer weight of numbers. He piggybacks on other hosts and uses their resources to increase his tribe. And in the right environment, he grows exponentially. A virus doesn't even have to mate — he just replicates, again and again with geometrically increasing power, doubling with each iteration:

1
11
1111
11111111
1111111111111111111111111111111

In a few short generations, a virus population can explode.

Viral Marketing Defined

What does a virus have to do with marketing? Viral marketing describes any strategy that encourages individuals to pass on a marketing message to others, creating the potential for exponential growth in the message's exposure and influence. Like viruses, such strategies take advantage of rapid multiplication to explode the message to thousands, to millions.

Off the Internet, viral marketing has been referred to as "word-of-mouth," "creating a buzz," "leveraging the media," "network marketing." But on the Internet, for better or worse, it's called "viral marketing." While others smarter than I have attempted to rename it, to somehow domesticate and tame it, I won't try. The term "viral marketing" has stuck.

The Classic Hotmail.com Example

The classic example of viral marketing is Hotmail.com, one of the first free Web-based email services. The strategy is simple:

Give away free email addresses and services, attach a simple tag at the bottom of every free message sent out: "Get your private, free email at *http://www.hotmail.com*," and, then stand back while people email to their own network of friends and associates, who see the message, sign up for their own free email service, and then propel the message still wider to their own ever-increasing circles of friends and associates. Like tiny waves spreading ever farther from a single pebble dropped into a pond, a carefully designed viral marketing strategy ripples outward extremely rapidly.

Elements of a Viral Marketing Strategy

Accept this fact. Some viral marketing strategies work better than others, and few work as well as the simple Hotmail.com strategy. But below are the six basic elements you hope to include in your strategy. A viral marketing strategy need not contain *all* these elements, but the more elements it embraces, the more powerful the results are likely to be. An effective viral marketing strategy:

- Gives away valuable products or services
- Provides for effortless transfer to others
- Scales easily from small to very large
- Exploits common motivations and behaviors
- Utilizes existing communication networks
- Takes advantage of others' resources

Let's examine each of these elements briefly.

1. Gives Away Valuable Products or Services

"Free" is the most powerful word in a marketer's vocabulary. Most viral marketing programs give away valuable products or services to attract attention. Free email services, free information, free "cool" buttons, free software programs that perform powerful functions but not as much as you get in the "pro" version. Wilson's Second Law of Web Marketing is "The Law of Giving and Selling" (*www.wilsonweb.com/wmta /basic-principles.htm*). "Cheap" or "inexpensive" may generate a wave of interest, but "free" will usually do it much faster. Viral marketers practice delayed gratification. They may not profit today, or tomorrow, but if they can generate a groundswell of interest from something free, they know they will profit "soon and for the rest of their lives" (with apologies to "Casablanca"). Patience, my friends. Free attracts eyeballs. Eyeballs then see other desirable things that you are selling, and, presto! you earn money. Eyeballs bring valuable email addresses, advertising revenue, and e-commerce sales opportunities. Give away something; sell something.

2. Provides for Effortless Transfer to Others

Public health nurses offer sage advice at flu season: stay away from people who cough, wash your hands often, and don't touch your eyes, nose, or mouth. Viruses only spread when they're easy to transmit. The medium that carries your marketing message must be easy to transfer and replicate: email, website, graphic, software download. Viral marketing works famously on the Internet because instant communication has become so easy and inexpensive. Digital format make copying simple. From a marketing standpoint, you must simplify your marketing message so it can be transmitted easily and without degradation. Short is better. The classic is: "Get your private, free email at *http://www.hotmail.com.*" The message is compelling, compressed, and copied at the bottom of every free email message.

3. Scales Easily from Small to Very Large

To spread like wildfire the transmission method must be rapidly scalable from small to very large. The weakness of the Hotmail model is that a free email service requires its own mail servers to transmit the message. If the strategy is wildly successful, mail servers must be added very quickly or the rapid growth will bog down and die. If the virus multiplies only to kill the host before spreading, nothing is accomplished. So long as you have planned ahead of time how you can add mail servers rapidly you're okay. You must build in scalability to your viral model.

4. Exploits Common Motivations and Behaviors

Clever viral marketing plans take advantage of common human motivations. What proliferated "Netscape Now" buttons in the early days of the Web? The desire to be cool. Greed drives people. So does the hunger to be popular, loved, and understood. The resulting urge to communicate produces millions of websites and billions of email messages. Design a marketing strategy that builds on common motivations and behaviors for its transmission, and you have a winner.

5. Utilizes Existing Communication Networks

Most people are social. Nerdy, basement-dwelling computer science grad students are the exception. Social scientists tell us that each person has a network of eight to twelve people in their close network of friends, family, and associates. People's broader networks may consist of scores, hundreds, or thousands of people, depending upon their position in society. A waitress, for example, may communicate regularly with hundreds of customers in a given week. Network marketers have long understood the power of these human networks, both the strong, close networks as well as the weaker networked relationships. People on the Internet develop networks of relationships, too. They collect email addresses and favorite website URLs. Affiliate programs exploit such networks, as do permission email lists. Learn to place your message into existing communications between people, and you rapidly multiply its dispersion.

6. Takes Advantage of Others' Resources

The most creative viral marketing plans use others' resources to get the word out. Affiliate programs, for example, place text or graphic links on others' websites. Authors who give away free articles seek to position their articles on others' web pages. A news release can be picked up by hundreds of periodicals and form the basis of articles seen by hundreds of thousands of readers. Now someone else's newsprint or webpage is relaying your marketing message. Someone else's resources are depleted rather than your own.

Put into Practice

Viral marketing is (fairly) easy to define, but very difficult to accomplish successfully. Marketing Sherpa's How to Viral Market toolkit is the best book available on the nuts and bolts of developing a successful viral marketing campaign. Strongly recommended for serious marketers.

◆ ◆ ◆

Almost by definition, viral marketing is impossible to predict or produce. It is, in some ways, like the Spirit that Jesus compared to the wind (John 3:8), which is beyond our control. The wind can be harnessed and has great power. So too we can be creative and craft our communication in such a way that if the Spirit decided to blow it around the world, it would be effective.

It's All about the Experience

Effective communication always creates or evokes an experience. How often have you preached a sermon and had people walk out having heard something you never said because you reminded them of the truth they knew all along?

Richard Reising, in his great book *Church Marketing 101*, talks about how Starbucks is not selling coffee; they are selling you an experience. They actually are trying to become America's front porch. He also cites the advertising of Mountain Dew (you can see the ads on YouTube), which does not try to tell you what the soft drink tastes like; they attempt to communicate who they want their market to be. Who knows what it tastes like, but they have succeeded in making it the preferred drink of young men in a certain demographic who want to "Do the Dew."

What would people actually experience if they came to your church?

- ◆ Unconditional welcome?
- ◆ Challenge to become more?
- ◆ Hope for their future?
- ◆ Nurturing for their family?
- ◆ Exciting music?
- ◆ Transformational truth effectively communicated?

- ◆ The living God from whom they came?
- ◆ Confidence in the God to whom they are going?

Do your website, emails, logo, ads, newsletter, buildings, people all consistently, persistently, and effectively communicate what it is you want people to experience when they come to your church? It isn't just that you want your communication to reflect and express that experience with integrity; you must begin to think of communication as a tool for shaping that experience.

A young man playing racquetball was losing badly. He was more athletic and skilled than his opponent, but something was wrong with his foot. After the match, as the young man limped off the court in defeat, the older man asked if he had injured himself. The young man replied, "No, I don't think so, but something must be wrong with my right foot because it doesn't fit my shoe very well."

The older man said, "Don't you mean something must be wrong with the shoe."

"No," he answered. "It must be my foot because these are Nike court shoes."

The marketing of Nike had been so effective that he discounted his own experience. Effectively marketing our churches can begin to shape the experience of those who give us a try. A contemporary, cutting-edge brand can help people look past our Gothic building and give us a chance. The question, of course, is will what they experience be as relevant and contemporary as our brand or as dated and dusty as our building?

One of my favorite resource-filled websites is "Church Marketing Sucks." Generally speaking, it really does, but it doesn't have to. We have a powerful and important story to tell. We have good news for people who desperately need it. What we haven't done so well is getting that good news outside our own walls.

These seven secrets all have focused on the things that we can do to proactively communicate to our community and congregation. We also should acknowledge that we are not always able to control what gets communicated about us. Rumors can take off on the Internet and do great harm. The media is a major challenge that is beyond our control because it is not prone to report good news. However, if the story is a positive one, the media can provide your church with more exposure than you could ever afford to buy.

Every church has a story to tell, and news outlets, including newspapers, television, radio, and websites, will tell that story for free, if you'll let them. Did your holiday benevolence project touch more lives than ever before? Tell the story. Do you have a special guest speaker who is going to talk about peace and justice issues? Tell the story. Did you just elect a new senior pastor? Tell the story.

All of these things and more are pieces of good news that your community might want, and even need, to know. Issue a clear, concise press release (with no typos!) sharing the who, what, where, why, and when, as though you are a reporter. The better written it is, the more likely they will pick up the story. You can find email addresses online, oftentimes even finding the person who writes this kind of story. Send photos of the event, or your guest, or your new pastor. Make the reporter's job as easy as possible, and return phone calls promptly! Reporters will come to recognize you as someone they can rely on and start to turn to you as a source for stories, information, or quotes about a particular topic. When they do, be prepared! Before you call a reporter back, do a little research about the topic and have some talking points ready. Tell reporters what you want them to know, not what they think they need to know!

If a conflict in your church, or something negative yet untrue, reaches the press, the relationships you have established with reporters can help you weather the storm and share your side of the story. Each situation is different, and you want to approach them as such. Don't avoid the criticism, however. There should be nothing to hide, so say as much. Answer questions directly. Regardless of how you intend it, people perceive "No comment" to mean you are not telling the truth.

Effective twenty-first-century communication is vital for those churches seeking to share the good news in a culture drowning in bad. It is the mission and ministry of all our churches, and it is critical if the mainline church is to have a future. The need is great. The "product" — grace, compassion, community, transformation, hope, peace, love — is the best. The breakdown is in our delivery systems. People are desperate for the very things we offer. Allowing people to die of spiritual dehydration when we have a fountain of living water is unconscionable. We would never do it deliberately, but let us not do it by neglect.

FIVE

Transformational Community

I have never met a church that didn't list "friendliness" as one of its leading assets. I, however, have visited dozens where only the ushers spoke to me. One church insisted that hospitality was their greatest gift. The Sunday I visited, I wore the brightest orange sweater in creation, and the only person who spoke to me was an older man who asked if I'd mind getting out of "their" pew. (He did ask nicely and say please.)

In new congregations, folks have worked very hard for months to launch a new adventure. They have bonded over long discussions, hard work, risk-taking, and sacrifice. That kind of fellowship is powerful, and, regardless of how friendly they try to be, new folks never will have the experiences the "charter members" did. In long-term stable or declining churches, the entire congregation has connected in a way that makes them like an extended family (albeit, often a dysfunctional extended family). The history and threatened future binds them together, but it generally frightens newcomers.

Churches are, by definition, communities. Large churches are often a community of communities. In some cases, that is a good thing. Rarely, however, is it the kind of connection new people are seeking, nor is it transformational for those who are involved already. In the past, community took place in mainline congregations in natural ways:

- Multiple services, including Sunday night and midweek, offered opportunity for community. People ate together before or after evening services.

- ◆ My parents have been members of the same Sunday school class for forty years. Few people stay married that long these days.

- ◆ Men's and women's groups participated in activities together.

- ◆ Committees and boards often had the same membership for years.

Today none of that exists, and few churches have been deliberate about replacing the opportunities. From the start, the natural rhythm of the church has been "cell and celebration." The earliest church attended worship in the temple or synagogue and then gathered together in homes for study, prayer, and the breaking of bread. Today vital churches still follow that model. Once a week, everyone gathers to celebrate and worship. It is a party, so the more the merrier. Study and connection and prayer happen in small groups that generally meet in people's homes. Churches that try to force their weekly worship time to meet both needs generally do neither well.

Prayer

While worship should include prayer, if that is the sum of a congregation's prayer life it is little wonder there is such a tepid connection to God. In small groups, people can be authentic, honest, and vulnerable, without being exhibitionists or voyeurs. In intimate gatherings, people can spend the time that is needed to articulate the yearnings of their hearts and unpack the hurts that need to be healed. Then the group can get serious about praying. Time can be given so that every voice can be heard, including God's.

In addition, people make prayer lists that allow them to practice praying daily for one another, reimaging the group and the person's face and voice when the person made the request. This encourages the practice of daily prayer and keeps community alive between meetings.

Although there are worship services that are built around an experience of authentic prayer, most services only have time to say prayers, and pretending otherwise turns off people who are seeking authenticity above all. Prayer is critical to the health of a vital church but shouldn't be short-changed by pretending that what we do in worship is the prayer life of the church. Craft the prayers of worship so that they are beautiful and inspirational, but having people speak in a room in which they can't be heard, about situations and people visitors don't know, doesn't serve anyone well.

Don't neglect to pray for one another. Create times and places where that genuinely happens with intimacy and authenticity. While prayer has a vital place in worship, remember that, ultimately, worship is supposed to be focused on God, not us. It is perhaps the only time in the course of a week when we are not the center of our world. Beware that our prayer practices in worship don't negate that.

Many churches have found that small groups whose organizing purpose is prayer can be quite transformational. In one church the entire congregation is divided into what they call "Prayer Teams." They gather every other week, with half of the groups meeting one week and the other half the next. They meet at different times throughout the week, so that half the congregation is gathered in serious prayer each week. They begin with a short lesson, usually about prayer. Then they talk about world and national events and pray about these, with community and church needs following. They end with a third time of prayer when the members each have a chance to share needs they have or that they know about. Each member notes the person's name and request on a card. They have one final time of prayer and then leave covenanting to pray daily for one another and the other needs that have been raised. Not surprisingly, this church is attractive to spiritual seekers, and their emphasis on prayer has transformed a conflicted, declining congregation into what their local paper called, "A haven of peace where the sweet spirit of the people is palpable when you walk in the door."

While your congregation may not decide that everyone needs to be in a prayer group, there probably are some people who feel that need or call, so that could be one type of small group your congregation offers. An alternative may be to try this as an experiment for Lent, or as a disciplined preparation before launching a time of renewal or special mission or ministry. Even in groups where the focus is study, some other *lectio divino,* healing, social justice, or some other practice of the church, prayer should be a disciplined emphasis. While we offer few imperatives, I am convinced that the prayer life of small groups should be the undergirding of every new or renewing congregation.

Fellowship: It Can't Be Done Well by a Congregation

There are some things that are done better by entire congregations than by small groups. Celebration may be one of those. Having hundreds of people fill a room with songs of praise can take us into the very presence of God, but connecting on a personal and emotionally intimate level in a crowd is inappropriate and downright weird. Healthy people don't bare their souls in public unless they are seeking attention rather than healing. In small groups, though, where there are appropriate levels of trust and familiarity, we can find help and healing. Large groups having coffee together and talking about their kids' soccer teams or the pastor's new haircut is great, but it must not become a substitute for the *koinonia* (intimate communion) that was, and is, foundational to the church of Jesus Christ.

Remarkably, 25 percent of Americans report having no meaningful social support at all — not a single person in whom they can confide — according to "Social Isolation: A Modern Plague" on *psychologytoday.com.* More than half of all Americans report having no close confidants or friends outside their immediate family. The situation is much worse today than it was when similar data were gathered in 1985. At that time, only 10 percent of Americans were completely alone.

In his remarkable book *Bowling Alone,* Robert Putnam talks about how we have become increasingly disconnected from family, friends, neighbors, and our democratic structures. Putnam warns that our stock of social capital — the very fabric of our connections with each other — has plummeted, impoverishing our lives and communities. Drawing on evidence that includes nearly five hundred thousand interviews over the last quarter century, he showed that we sign fewer petitions, belong to fewer organizations that meet, know our neighbors less, meet with friends less frequently, and even socialize with our families less often. We're even bowling alone. More Americans are bowling than ever before, but they are not bowling in leagues. Putnam shows how changes in work, family structure, age, suburban life, television, computers, women's roles, and other factors have contributed to this decline. According to Putnam, for every ten minutes added to commute time, there is roughly a 10 percent decrease in social ties.

Ten years ago Putnam began raising the alarm about what would become of our society should this trend continue. The rancor and incivility of our political life, the dramatic decline in caring for the most vulnerable, the complete loss of interest in the quality of education for anyone's children other than our own, and the unwillingness to address long-term issues like the environment that will impact future generations — all are symptoms of the loss of community that our culture suffers currently. Salvation from this deadly relational epidemic is in the hands of the church. We always have been called to be co-redeemers of the world, and this is one of the tools the Spirit has given us.

"Fellowship" is an insipid word for a life-giving function of the church. Our goal should be nothing less than to ensure that every member has an opportunity and invitation to be a part of some small group where they can experience community. Not everyone needs us to provide them community. However, more people do than we think, and more people need community than think they do. One of our responsibilities is to educate people about this need.

In one church where I was pastor, we combined two programs that had been available long ago through the United Methodist Church. For Lent we invited everyone to participate in what we called "An Experiment in Practical Christianity." Since the original series was created by Candler School of Theology professors John and Adrienne Carr in the 1970s, we updated and adapted it to our more progressive setting. In the two months leading up to Lent, in every creative way we could think of, we advertised and promoted an appeal for "Twelve Brave Christians." (This phrase was borrowed from another small group renewal program from the 1970s.) We did everything in our power to recruit, coerce, motivate, and compel every member of the church to join a small group for the season of Lent and simply to participate in this "experiment in practical Christianity." The result was the transformation of a congregation. People who thought they would hate it realized how much was missing from their lives.

Out of this Lenten experiment, dozens of small groups were born that continued for years. The result was that the congregation grew in number remarkably fast. We discovered that by having a large number of small groups, visitors had plenty of opportunities to get connected quickly. In addition, people were very willing to invite a visitor or new member to come to their small group. Ultimately, though, the most powerful discovery was that, by integrating almost all the existing congregation into small groups, they were supportive of the growth of the church.

In hindsight, we realized that the loss of extended families that is so pervasive in our culture has made people treat the church as their extended family. Growth threatens them with the loss of that familial experience where they know and are known. In fact, growth is a more urgent threat than decline. The result is that in many single-cell churches someone inevitably will sabotage the growth of the congregation, not out of any nefarious motives but out of a subconscious fear of losing something precious.

In churches that provide multiple alternatives for authentic community, the existing congregation will be much more supportive of the growth of the church. This is as true in new churches as in existing ones. Do not underestimate the resistance that is rooted in the threatened loss of a sense of "family." Large and consistently growing churches have created mechanisms whereby members can keep their sense of family in the cells of the body and are therefore willing to invite others to the celebration without fear that something valuable will be lost if the church grows. Again, little of this is conscious, but then that is almost always true about our resistance to transformation, isn't it?

Formation/Education

While Bible churches organize around hour-long Bible lessons taught by the pastor, this isn't a selling point for most mainline Protestants. The didactic form of education that once took place in sermons and Sunday school classes simply doesn't work well for contemporary adults. As we take our spiritual journeys together, it is most valuable to provide opportunities for people to speak about their own experiences and to hear from peers what they are learning and feeling. In many emergent churches the sermon has been replaced with a conversation, which works well with the proper leadership. Whether this is a long-term development is yet to be seen; however, the number one fear in America is still public speaking. The result of that fear is that often the same voices are heard every time in public settings, and, let's be frank, the most functional people often don't speak up in larger groups.

Christian education for contemporary people is most effectively done in small groups, but in most churches the only education most adults get happens on Sunday morning. Faith formation in intimate communities during the week, coupled with an effective time of celebration on the weekend, has great power to change lives.

Actually, this rhythm of cell/celebration/service is the perfect model for spiritual formation. An individual is spiritually nurtured in small groups — as is the community — where they can learn and teach, grow and share together. Then they gather as a congregation of community for celebration where they are energized, challenged, inspired, and sent. Then they scatter to be the Body of Christ and serve those in need. It is the cycle of life for a healthy church.

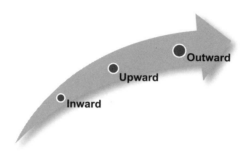

Education can take place in large groups, as Bishop Robert Schnase says in his *Five Practices of Fruitful Congregations:*

> As we mature in Christ, God cultivates in us the fruit of the spirit: "love, joy, peace, patience, kindness, generosity, faithfulness, gentleness, and self-control" (Gal. 5:22–23). These are the qualities to which the Christian aspires; these are the qualities God's Spirit forms in us as we deepen our relationship with God through Christ. These interior spiritual qualities are all radically relational, and we only learn them in the presence of others through the practice of love.

Bishop Schnase believes that what he calls "intentional faith development" is one of the secrets to a vital and vibrant congregation, and he is not alone. In her work on practicing congregations, Diana Butler Bass has discovered that in churches where spiritual formation is a practice renewal and growth are a natural outcome. This is not simply one of the many programs of the church; it is the essence of what we do as Christians: formation, worship, service. In *The Practicing Congregation*, she says, "In an age of fragmentation, it may well be the case that the vocation of the church is to turn tourists into pilgrims — those who no longer journey aimlessly, but rather those who journey in God and whose lives are mapped by the grace of Christian practices."

Kirk Hadaway, in *Behold I Do a New Thing*, suggests that formation is for children and transformation is for adults. I value his insights greatly, but with the secularization of our society, many of the adults who come to our churches have almost no spiritual background or education. For our existing congregations, the work in small groups may indeed be transformation, but, if our churches begin to attract more of those who are hungry for authentic spirituality, we must be prepared to do formation with adults, as well as children and youth.

Caring

In many churches the only opportunity for members even to see one another is on Sunday morning. The result is that many people feel the care of the congregation only when they see them or the pastor or staff before or after church. An elderly woman described her frustration this way:

> I finally just got mad. Every Sunday the pastor and all the people in my church checked on me to see how I was doing. Hell, I'd just lost the person I'd lived with for sixty years and the love of my life, how did they think I was doing? On Sunday morning I was doing fine, but where were they Thursday night when the furnace wouldn't light. I don't need hundreds of people to express support once a week. In the end it just makes it worse.

In a culture where we no longer live in extended families and neighbors are never even spoken to, creating a genuinely caring community can be powerful, one of our unique contributions to society. It is great to communicate on Facebook, but everyone needs time with other people if you want a hug. People do care, and small groups allow the average person an opportunity to show that they do. Today few churches are able to do such simple things like taking food to the sick or bereaved, but a small group is well able to care for its members. Thus, the church cares for all members better than the most hyperactive pastor ever could.

As progressives, we all value diversity, though few of our churches reflect that value very well. Small groups are often the places where homogeneity is appropriate. Although we must be careful of creating exclusive groups, congruent groups may be appropriate for lesbian, gay, bisexual, and transgender folks, or single mothers, or elderly widows, or families with children, or teenagers, or people who work downtown, or people in a twelve-step program. In all of these cases and others, people have unique needs, and people who share the same life experiences often are better able to meet those needs. A small group of people who share your life experience can offset feeling like an outsider or stranger in a congregation that is different and can't fully understand your situation.

Churches that utilize small groups to provide care discover that the professional staff is freed up for other responsibilities and the members are better cared for than in churches where an employee is paid to care. That is harshly worded deliberately so that we might recall that the role of the pastor is not to be the church, but to equip the members to be the church. Although it requires a shift in thinking for existing churches, once members realize that their role is to care for one another, it actually is a bit frightening for the pastor to appear in your hospital room. Small groups ensure more effective and consistent care and less necessary pastoral care. The biggest obstacle is often the pastor who easily can become attached to the self-image of "hero in a crisis." When a family says that they want the small group leader to officiate at their loved one's funeral, the pastor will know that he or she has done a good job "equipping the saints."

Service

Healthy churches often say that they do only three things: worship, small groups, and community service. That is great, but even service can be done through small groups. There are some projects that require the combined efforts of the entire congregation, like mission projects or building a Habitat for Humanity house. Even some of these larger tasks, though, can be accomplished best by mobilizing people in their cells of community. The entire church may feed the homeless every Saturday, but it may be much easier to get dependable volunteers if the cells each take a Saturday a month. On a cold Saturday morning, it is tempting to sleep in, but your peers, not to mention hungry people, are counting on you and will give you grief if you are a no-show. Churches have a tough time holding people accountable for their commitments, but friends and neighbors can ridicule you into compliance. (Just kidding, but there is a grain of truth in that.)

Each small group needs to have a service ministry, lest it become ingrown and self-absorbed. A member may know of a single mother who is unemployed but too embarrassed to ask the church for help. The small group can work together to help without demeaning someone who already is struggling. In the process, those who give and serve and help genuinely are transformed because they are able to live like the Body of Christ for no motive other than it was the right thing to do.

When people say, "I'm going to church" what they almost always mean is that they are going to attend a worship service at which they will be mostly a passive recipient. Imagine if that phrase came to mean, "I'm going to a small group where I can be authentic and intimate and give others grace to do the same, where I can pray and be prayed for, where I can learn and share a little of what I know, where I can care and be cared for, and where I can serve in a way that doesn't benefit me except to help me find my purpose for living." If *that* was what it meant to "go to church" our churches would be exploding in growth. What I just described is what every human needs. Your church can provide a great gift by simply facilitating those kinds of transformational communities.

If the principal mission of our small group ministry is spiritual formation/transformation, it is imperative that each cell has service projects throughout the year. This is one of the key ways we can turn our church inside out and make it externally oriented. If these service projects are recognized, honored, and even supported by the entire church, there is a sense of ownership and identity that comes, as it should, with members of the larger body living out the call of Christ. Every church has had the experience of having a need go unmet because no one would volunteer. If, however, the pastor calls a small group leader and asks if her or his cell would be willing to tackle a project, then a dozen or so volunteers are mobilized immediately.

We have been talking about small groups in general, but there are some specific alternatives. For example, the board, council, vestry, or consistory has a specific function that usually is outlined by the church's constitution or bylaws. The work that they do could be considered their service or ministry. However, if other small groups are studying a particular topic or book, the leadership team could use part of their time to do some study as well. If one member of the leadership team is ill, the rest of the team is likely to visit that member in the hospital or at home. Formalizing this function helps the governance team to see their work as another ministry of the church and to experience it in a spiritual context. The altar guild or tenors or house-and-grounds team also could be organized as a cell in the body.

Seeing the church as a body made up of cells can help give this aspect of the church's life the kind of energy, attention, and leadership it deserves because it is a basic building block for the health of the body. Rather than forming a committee or a team to accomplish a task, think in terms of cells. A parents' cell group can be a major asset to the youth group or children's ministry. A "Renewed Life" group actually may be a twelve-step group that follows the principles of other twelve-step groups but members name their higher power. The epicurean cell may meet once a month to have dinner at a different restaurant and then write a review for the church newsletter. The study and sharing of prayer requests may happen virtually on a nonpublic Facebook page or other website. The possibilities are endless, but the perspective is that the entire church rests on the three legs of cell, celebration, and service.

The key to making this a powerful and effective ministry is, of course, the small group leaders. The beginning point is to remind people that Jesus didn't change the world by being elected to an office; rather, he chose twelve people with whom to share his life's journey. Small group leaders must be the VIPs to the pastor because, ultimately, they are the women and men charged with the care and feeding of the souls of the congregation. In an ideal situation, the pastor sees the small group leaders as their cell to recruit, guide, care for, and mentor. The pastor may not visit every member of the church who is ill, but the small group leaders are the people for whom the pastor is responsible. The pastor cares for them and strengthens them to care for their members.

These leaders are carefully chosen and personally trained. If you are starting six small groups then twelve leaders must be recruited. You will need six leaders and six co-leaders. Or you may select six leaders and ask them to find an "apprentice." Each small group has two leaders who share responsibility. As members of the group invite others to join them and as new people join the church, the small groups hopefully grow in numbers. Eventually they will have outgrown the living room of the home in which they meet. When that happens, like any healthy cell, the small group multiplies. The "apprentice" then becomes the leader of the new group and both leaders seek new apprentices. The natural creation of new cell groups is important because they are the place where new people will fit in most easily.

The leaders don't need to be people who are biblical experts or experienced teachers. With each new study, the pastor or responsible staff or leader will gather the leaders and work with them through the material with them. In the end, the small group leaders are trained continually to be skilled facilitators, not subject-matter experts. Beyond the material provided, the expertise must arise from the group. Following are the very succinct guidelines provided to Circle of Hope (small group) leaders at the Cathedral of Hope UCC:

Guidelines for Group Facilitators

You can help create a positive atmosphere in a circle where everyone will want to participate. Here's how:

1. Retain the focus of the group. The focus of the group is spiritual growth. Circles are neither therapy groups nor matchmaking groups.

2. Attend faithfully. Your faithful attendance shows you care about the other circle members and you want the circle to function well.

3. Prepare before the meetings. Read the lesson plan and answer the questions in your own mind before coming to the circle meeting.

4. Show interest in others. Give your full attention to the person who is sharing.

5. Don't judge. Respect the point of view of others in the circle.

6. Don't preach. Encourage others to express their own ideas.

7. Use humor. Try to keep the tone of the discussion fun and enjoyable unless the lesson plan material calls for something different.

8. Seek balanced participation. Share your ideas and feelings, but never allow anyone (including yourself) to dominate the discussion.

9. Confess no one's deficiencies but your own. When discussing a personal problem, do not confess the sins of others.

10. Maintain confidentiality. Whatever is shared in the group must be kept within the group.

11. Keep the personal touch. Share honestly and specifically, avoiding generalities.

Keeping these guidelines in mind will make your time together much more productive.

Below is a sample lesson plan for the first meeting of a new small group. It includes the covenant that each small group (circle) member is asked to make and keep.

THE COVENANT OF A NEW COMMUNITY
by Dan Peeler, Minister for Children and Families,
Cathedral of Hope UCC, Dallas

1. Begin this first meeting with individual introductions. You might ask people to share basic information. Keep it simple. There will be plenty of time to get to know one another. One of the leaders should begin and model what you are asking them to do. The other leader should go last.

   + Name

   + Occupation or interests.

   + Member of Cathedral of Hope? How long?

2. In future weeks, we will be getting together to have some social times and some discussions based on lesson plans from the church, but tonight is a group consecration and get-acquainted night. We're also going to talk about new communities and the covenants that keep them together. How would anyone define a "covenant"? (A promise, sometimes unconditional, between God and humankind, sometimes a mutual agreement between people.)

3. Icebreaker: Both Testaments of the Bible are full of covenants and covenant language, beginning with God's covenants with Adam and Eve, Cain, Noah, and all of creation, Sarah and Abraham, Rebecca, Jacob, entire tribes and entire nations. God was in the habit of making and never breaking promises.

Following that divine model, we also have covenants between human individuals: Jonathan and David; Jacob and Esau; Ruth and Naomi; Jesus and his disciples; the early church with one another. (Break into groups of two or three and discuss for about five minutes the most important promises you ever made. Follow with sharing time among the entire group.)

4. Listen to this reading from Acts 2, verses 43–47:

> Awe came upon everyone, because many wonders and signs were being done by the apostles. All who believed were together and had all things in common; they would sell their possessions and goods and distribute the proceeds to all, as any had need. Day by day, as they spent much time together in the temple, they broke bread at home and ate their food with glad and generous hearts, praising God and having the goodwill of all the people. And day by day the Lord added to their number.

Think of some things we, as a new group, might have in common with this picture of the first gatherings of the early church. (Encourage responses. Discussion points are below.)

- They had things in common outside of their belief system.

- They shared in distributing possessions and funds for the common good (as we do in various programs of the church).

- They spent time together at their homes outside of church (temple) having meetings (praising God) and sharing food.

- They were friends to one another. (They shared genuine affection and openness, as we will learn as the Book of Acts continues to tell their story.)

5. In a time of cyber-centered methods of communication, there is a major need for people to get together in person in order to form real friendships and to learn to trust one another. In

his book *The Origins of Love and Hate,* psychologist Ian Suttie suggests:

> Our major repression today is not of sexual or aggressive impulses, but of affection and openness. We can't get enough of what we don't really want: things. But what is needed and wanted is emotional closeness. Not sex, nor food, nor power, nor any other surrogate can satisfy that need.

In some of the longtime circles of this church, there are people who testify that their circle friends are among the closest, if not *the* closest, relationships of their entire lives. Get into your groups again, with new people this time if you can, and tell about some individuals from small groups that made a difference in your past. What drew you together? What made you feel comfortable with them? (Three or four minutes, and then share a few stories with the entire group again.)

6. Now back to the covenant talk we had earlier: all groups of any kind function best together when they share an agreed-upon set of promises, which this church likes to call "covenants." Here's a handout (on the following page) about circle covenants, which we will go over together. (Pass out the provided copies.) This is for group discussion, so please ask questions or make comments as we read through it.

7. Discuss group consensus about meeting times and potluck or refreshment decisions. After the discussion, pass around paper for email addresses, and ask for volunteers to cover some of the above-mentioned duties.

8. Ask about group prayer needs or praises. Close with circle prayer. In a circle prayer, all members join hands, and the member to the leader's right starts the prayer time or squeezes the hand of the next person if they choose to pass. This process continues around the circle and back to the leader, who closes the prayer time.

◆ ◆ ◆

COVENANT FOR INDIVIDUAL MEMBERS
INVOLVED IN CIRCLE MINISTRY

- To make regular meeting attendance a priority. (Meetings can be weekly, biweekly or monthly. The meeting schedule is set up according to individual group covenants.)
- To encourage and build up other members.
- To discover and utilize your spiritual gifts.
- To better discern God's direction for your lives.
- To participate in group ministry projects.
- To prayerfully consider your own gifts as a possible future circle leader.
- To feel comfortable in inviting guests to meetings.
- To understand the circle leader should not be expected to provide for all the circle's needs, and, therefore, . . .
- To share responsibilities in:
  - Sending email reminders of meeting times.
  - Making phone calls.
  - Helping with child care (if needed).
  - Providing various hospitality and social planning services.
  - Bringing refreshments or covered dish contributions, according to the circle's decided food arrangements.
- To support the church through regular attendance and other covenant fulfillments. (We realize there will be visitors brought into the circle who do not attend the church. This is a general suggestion.)
- To participate in circle discussions.
- To scrupulously maintain a covenant of confidentiality concerning any personal sharing during group discussions and to make this agreement known to any guests brought to a meeting.
- To set aside regular times of prayer for other members.

There are many sources of material for small groups to study. Many mainline churches have had good experience using the *Living the Questions* series of videos. Others find books with discussion questions at the end of each chapter helpful. Still others gather to study the lectionary lessons, either in preparation for the coming Sunday or in response to what they just experienced. The groups are generally free to decide for themselves what they will study or how they will function.

You may ask leaders to reserve certain seasons or time periods, like Lent or September–November, so that the entire church might study together. It is very effective if the pastor has prepared far enough in advance to allow the small group studies to connect with what is happening on Sunday mornings. Some churches eventually develop a curriculum circle. This is often made up of seminary graduates, educators, or insightful teachers who gather to write and develop resources. They, too, function as a circle. One other function this serves is that, when "experts" attend regular small group meetings, the average person often falls silent because they assume another knows more than they do. These kinds of specialized small groups allow people with education and experience to contribute without dominating.

Every group, family, congregation, staff, and community has members who challenge the dynamics and functioning of the group. Bill Eure (longtime partner of Michael Piazza) was one of the original founders of the small group movement that enabled the Cathedral of Hope UCC to grow into the largest progressive church in the South. He has written two small group exercises, that are included at the end of this book. He also developed a couple of very practical documents for the Cathedral of Hope that we thought might be helpful to you or those who lead your small group ministry. The first is set of guidelines for dealing with challenging persons in a small group.

HOW TO DEAL WITH SPECIAL PEOPLE
by Bill Eure

EGRs

Some people come to circle meetings with some very special problems in their lives. One such type is what are known as EGRs (Extra Grace Required). Carl George, in his book *Prepare Your Church for the Future,* describes this situation:

> Many lay people have led groups in which a misbehaving member destroyed the experience for everyone. This EGR person (Extra Grace Required) seems to have a hole in his or her soul. Although an entire group pours in all the love they can find, an EGR will still complain, blame, and demand more. No matter how much acceptance small groups show, EGRs will use the gathering as an explosive courtroom-style hearing to play out their hurt and sickness, rather than to find healing. Such a person has extra needs stemming from a personal crisis, fragmented family, dysfunctional childhood, or medical neurosis. Some of these hurting members are bottomless wells who can siphon off all the love, interest, and energy an entire group can offer.

As soon as you identify an EGR, the circle leader should notify the coach. (*In this setting, the coach was the resource person for the small group leaders.*) Together, the coach and leader will agree on a plan of action, which may include some or all of the following:

+ Discuss the situation with the pastor.
+ Meet with the EGR to discuss needs and options.
+ Refer the EGR for counseling.
+ Remove the EGR from the group.

All of these plans of action must be done with care and concern for the person in need. Even though circle meetings can be therapeutic, they are not therapy groups. The most loving thing we can do for special needs persons may be to assist them in finding the appropriate group or setting for their needs. Remember that they are persons of sacred worth beloved by God and treasured by us all. However, so is everyone else in the group, and everyone's needs ought not to go unmet because the group is not designed or equipped to meet the special needs of one person. Sometimes the extra grace that is required is the grace to say, "No."

Antagonists

Kenneth C. Haugk defines antagonists in his book *Antagonists in the Church: How to Identify and Deal with Destructive Conflict:*

> Antagonists are individuals who, on the basis of nonsubstantive evidence, go out of their way to make insatiable demands, usually attacking the person or performance of others. These attacks are selfish in nature, tearing down rather than building up, and are frequently directed against those in a leadership capacity.

If someone in the circle seems antagonistic, ask yourself the following questions:

- Is the person's behavior disruptive?
- Is the attack irrational?
- Does the person go out of the way to initiate trouble?
- Are the person's demands insatiable?
- Are the concerns upon which the persons base the attack minimal or fabricated?
- Does the person avoid causes that involve personal risk, suffering, or sacrifice?
- Does the person's motivation appear selfish?
- Is the energy disproportionate to the issue or inappropriate to the setting?
- Is this an isolated incident of a pattern that is harming the group?

If someone in the circle is genuinely antagonistic, the leader needs to involve the coach or pastor immediately. Together they will agree on a plan of action. One of the leader's jobs is to protect the circle from harm or destructive behaviors. Unlike EGRs, who usually can be handled very gently, antagonists may have to be dealt with firmly and consistently by all involved. While very rarely are they physically dangerous, they may be emotionally dangerous to vulnerable people who have covenanted to be open and honest.

Seekers

One of the circle's greatest opportunities is to bring new people into the church. As these people come into the circle, however, there are several points that leaders need to keep in mind. These "seekers" may be entering a "church" situation for the first time in a long time or ever. They may have had little or no exposure to Christian faith, behaviors, or small group dynamics. Their previous experience with Christianity may have been negative. Exploring their spirituality may be a new and frightening experience for them. Seekers need to be treated gently, with respect and understanding. The following may help you be more sensitive in your dealings with seekers:

- Be aware that they may not share your perspective or have any real knowledge of scripture, doctrine, or faith. Make concepts clear enough for them to understand, and avoid all insider language.

- Understand that they may be somewhat nervous or skeptical. Never push them or put them on the spot. Let them have a chance to observe. At this point, it is good that they are at least attending.

- Be careful never to criticize "non-Christians" or other faiths. This is not how we do things anyway, but, for seekers, intolerance may be something they already associate with "Christians."

- Always be willing to share *your* faith and *your* beliefs, but never try to force others to believe like you. Openness to diversity of faith experience is a key feature of the circle and our church.

+ Encourage seekers to attend church with the group, to read appropriate books, and to continue to come to the circle, but do not force them to do so. Don't belittle or embarrass them if they don't do things the way you want them to.

+ As seekers become more interested in exploring their own faith journeys, encourage them to talk with you and others in the circle about their ideas and faith experiences. Tell them the pastors are also available if they have further questions.

Helping seekers discover their faith is one of the primary reasons the circle exists. You are in a unique position to help a seeker become a disciple.

◆ ◆ ◆

Finally, a word about small group multiplication. This is one of the healthiest and most life-giving processes in any church. It is also one of the most difficult. Again, Bill Eure has helped us by providing a guiding document for multiplication:

SMALL GROUP MULTIPLICATION
by Bill Eure

Multiplication is the way that circles maintain their health and their growth. It is sometimes an anxious process for most circles to go through, especially the first time. Those circles, however, that have been through the multiplication process agree that the benefits of multiplication far outweigh the fears some have about it.

When the number of regular attendees in a circle reaches ten to twelve, the circle leader and apprentice should begin the process of preparing the circle for multiplication. This includes having new apprentices in mind and ready to serve. Additionally, it is important to begin talking about multiplication within the circle meeting. This helps people get used to the idea and also gives them a chance to raise their questions and express their fears. Multiplication must happen when a circle has fifteen regular participants. Some of the most common fears about multiplication (and how you can respond to them) include:

- "We'll miss our friends." Remind the group that they will see each other in church and on other occasions. Also, it is helpful to plan a "joint circle social" in the near future where the two circles can gather for a meal, a party or an outing. This reminds them that not meeting together in a circle does not shut people off from their lives.

- "We don't want to multiply." Circles exist to multiply. Multiplication means there's always room for new friends to come to a circle. This is the evangelistic part of being a circle. Also, the intimacy level drops dramatically when a group gets too big. The things that are so special about being part of a circle — a chance to share deep feelings, bonding with a small group, hearing people's stories, etc. — does not happen as well in a large group.

- "We won't invite new people to circle so we won't have to multiply." Groups who have tried this report what devastating effects this has on the health of the circle. New people are the lifeblood of the circle. They remind us that one of the goals of a healthy circle is to make room for one more new person. New people bring their own insights and stories, which offer a new perspective on the lesson plans. Our circles are designed to never be closed. They are not exclusive clubs, but places where people can come and learn about God and their faith.

The circle ministry of our church is about disciples making disciples. By allowing our circles to grow and multiply, we are ministering actively to, and making disciples of, more and more people of God. Just as the bond that formed in the beginning made the circle so special for the initial people in the group, a new bond will be just as special for the circle as it changes and multiplies.

The circle leader and apprentice must model an excitement and positive outlook about multiplication. The circle will look to you for leadership on this. Your attitude will set the tone for how successful the multiplication will be.

Multiplication Methods

There are several ways to multiply. The leader and apprentice should discuss with their coach the plan they decide to use. Any of them can be successful with the right preparation.

- The apprentice (A1) chooses a new apprentice (A2) plus a couple of others who become the new circle. This method leaves most of the circle intact. This method is good if the A1 and the new circle have a specialized ministry to pursue as a circle. This also can be useful if the A1 is trying to plant a circle in a specific geographic area so that those people who live in that area multiply with the A1.

- The circle leader chooses new apprentice (A2) plus a couple of others who become the new circle. This is a variation on the first option, except that the A1 becomes the leader of the original circle.

- The leader and A1 choose from among the circle who will be in each new circle. This method can be useful if the circle has a great deal of confidence in the leader and the A1. There should always be the option for circle members to move to the other circle if the one they are placed in does not work for them.

- Selection of new circle members is done by lot. This method has been used successfully by several circles. Again, people are given the option of moving if they are absolutely unhappy with where they end up.

If your circle is having difficulty deciding how to multiply, ask your coach for assistance. Remember, just like in the human body, cells either multiply or they die. Healthy, living, growing, multiplying cells (circles) are the building blocks of our church.

◆ ◆ ◆

That final reminder is important for all aspects of the church. Change and growth are signs of health, vitality, and new life. Stagnation, resistance to change, and continuing unproductive patterns are clear signs of the absence of the Spirit. Remember the analogy of the funeral home and children's nursery. One is quiet, clean, sterile, and orderly. The other is noisy, frantic, and chaotic. We may not relish all the challenges that come from a comprehensive small group ministry, but neither do we want to fearlessly lead a mortuary.

SIX

Born Pregnant

Stardate: 4523.3. Captain James T. Kirk and his crew are called to Deep Space Station K7 by a priority-one distress call. The station is near Sherman's Planet, a world in a sector of space disputed between the Federation and the Klingon Empire. Under the terms of the Organian Peace Treaty, Sherman's Planet would be awarded to whichever side demonstrates that it can manage it more efficiently.

Kirk is furious when he realizes later that the distress call was unwarranted, and the undersecretary in charge of agriculture in the sector, Nilz Baris, simply wants someone to guard the shipments of quadrotriticale, a four-lobed wheat-rye hybrid grain, bound for Sherman's Planet. To Baris's annoyance, Kirk assigns two token guards to the task shortly before learning that Starfleet Command endorses Baris's concerns. Meanwhile, an independent trader, Cyrano Jones, brings some little furry animals called tribbles onto the station to sell; he gives one to Lieutenant Uhura as a marketing ploy. She brings it on board the Enterprise, where it and its offspring are treated as adorable pets. The animals purr a relaxing trill that the crew (even the stoic Mr. Spock) find soothing. The "trouble" with the tribbles is that they reproduce far too quickly and are capable of eating a planet barren if their breeding is not controlled. In the words of Dr. McCoy, "They are born pregnant."

This episode of the short-lived original *Star Trek* television series is an important reminder that the church of Jesus Christ was born pregnant. One of the priorities of new churches in the Book of Acts was to assist in the birth of other new churches. It was a part of their DNA. Like the tribbles, it appears they were born pregnant.

Committees vs. Teams

This seems to be a good model for every ministry of the church as well. As a church moves from committees to teams, one of the differentiating factors ought to be that teams multiply. As the work expands, a team can multiply into two teams to lead different aspects of the task. This happens because, from the very beginning, a team is gathered, not appointed and approved. Under the old model, a nominating committee would beg, cajole, and compel people to serve on various committees within the church. Then they had to be "approved" by the council or congregation. As soon as their term was over, they were gone, often from the church. The opposite problem also could arise: committees become closed communities from which the same people or families run the church for years. Either way is deadly.

What would your church look like if you abolished all committees and created ministry teams? These teams would:

- Exist only if their function is vital and needed, and only for as long as their function is vital and needed. From the very start, they are given permission to do their job and then "go out of business."

- Be composed of people who feel called to serve. Of course, calls are as different as the individuals, but those who have a concern, an interest, or a talent in a particular area might be encouraged to serve as volunteers on that team. No one has to approve them, because, after all, who are we to judge the call of the Spirit?

- Serve, work, and minister, *not* manage. There would be no motions or votes or minutes. The mission of a team is to get a job done, not to make decisions. When choices must be made, the group works to a consensus, with everyone agreeing to function as a team.

- Remember from the start that one of their functions is to multiply. That may mean that they help give birth to new ministries or midwife a new mission when theirs is complete. It must always mean that they are responsible for multiplying their own ministry by recruiting others to join the team and mentoring new folks who share their passion.

Leaders Give Birth to Leaders

Leaders mentoring leaders is how "discipleship" always has worked. Read the stories of the Book of Acts again. When Paul set out to answer a call, he never went alone. He always chose one or two people to go along so that they might learn and be able to do the work as well. This may mean that we need to train our leaders from the start to see training their successor as one of their crucial functions. Jesus sent the disciples out two by two. Although it doesn't say this, I wonder if he did not pair them as mentors and apprentices. All mature persons owe it to the Body of Christ to share what they have learned.

In control-oriented churches leadership is defined by position. You are a leader because someone has appointed you or voted on you and put you in authority. While we delude ourselves into thinking these positions have power, they rarely accomplish much of significance other than maintaining a diminishing organization. What if "leader" was defined as someone who has a passion and willingness to gather others together with a similar passion; as someone willing to be a part of a team who is doing something that helps the Reign of God to come "on earth as it is in heaven"? What if leaders were those who assisted others to follow their passion and answer their life's call? True leaders may hold no office or position. They are people who get something done and empower others to do the same. True leaders multiply their effectiveness by mentoring, encouraging, and inspiring others. They are never soloists or, as John Maxwell is so fond of saying, 'He who thinketh he leadeth but hath no followers is merely taking a walk."

Multiply, Don't Divide

In a congregation that is wired or being rewired for growth, small groups are created with multiplication in mind. Every class or small group has both a leader and an apprentice. Often when people are asked to lead a small group, they will say that they "aren't ready" or don't know enough. They aren't refusing, but they also don't deserve to be thrust into a role for which they do not yet have the confidence. They are perfect candidates to be apprentices. It may be that they will learn a great deal by having an experienced wiser leader show them the ropes. It also may be that they realize that leadership isn't such a mystery after all, and they can do it too.

The small group should be formed with the idea that others always are welcomed into the family. In fact, everyone should ever be on the lookout for people whose lives might be enriched by participating in an intimate spiritual community. While visiting a new church might be intimidating, accompanying a friend to a small gathering is something most people can manage. Small groups should be seen as side doors into the church. In some churches that do this exceptionally well more people attend their small groups each week than attend worship. In one church in Jacksonville, Florida, these small groups even received an offering and more donations were made there than during worship. The point is that an organizing principle for every new small group should be proactive hospitality: everyone is welcome, and, if our lives are being enriched by this experience, it is rude not to share it.

Of course, if the group is effective and people do invite others, it soon will become too large for the living room in which it meets. The day will come when the group must multiply. The apprentice will lead the new group.

Small group multiplication is an art, and there are other resources for explaining how it is done effectively. The principle here is that if we create small groups and other ministries with an orientation toward growth, they can multiply the number of people we can serve. Every small group should be "born pregnant." Even closed groups like twelve-step programs understand the need to welcome others in need. As a result, their orientation also should be to grow because there are lots of unmet needs out there. We don't divide the Body of Christ, but healthy cells in a body always reproduce through multiplication.

Churches Birthing Churches

To state the obvious: cats give birth to cats, and elephants give birth to elephants. Why then should it be a surprise that new churches are birthed by existing churches? It has been so since the beginning. Acts is a long description of how the Spirit gave birth to the church in Jerusalem, and, from then on, churches were started by other churches. The story often is recorded as the work of an individual, but Paul's epistles show how existing churches supported the birthing of new congregations.

This also has been the reality of our own history. Most of the congregations in American Protestantism were birthed through the work of existing congregations. That is likely to be true of the church where you are a member today. With very little effort, you probably could trace your congregation's genealogy back to the handful of congregations that were formed in this country because churches in Europe sent people or missionaries or money. Even in more recent history, churches starting churches has been the common practice.

Unfortunately, the values that gave rise to that impetus for so many years seem to have disappeared from the vision and value of most contemporary mainline Protestant congregations. In the United Church of Christ, for example, churches planting churches probably numbers in the single digits. Given the decline of the mainline, almost all of our energy and resources have been diverted to survival, which, ironically, has only hastened our demise.

The result has been that the responsibility for starting new congregations has shifted to the denominational and middle judicatory levels, which have accrued an appalling track record of expensive failure. This is not their fault; it was a systemic approach that was mistaken. The verdict is in: churches give birth to churches. While denominational bureaucracy is completely competent to serve the church in many ways, planting new congregations is not one of them. In recent years, the result of their efforts has been expensive plants that rarely have thrived. On the other hand, churches formed by other churches have a greater chance for survival, require a significantly lower startup cost, and become self-sustaining much more quickly. The denomination's role, as it has always been, is to support, encourage, and resource these efforts that arise from the passion of a local church.

Yes, humans give birth to humans, but, despite some resemblances, all parents know that the lives of their children are very different. So too as we set out on this adventure of the Spirit, we must make peace with the fact that what is born is likely to be very different from what we envisioned originally. In fact, it might be helpful to consider the possibilities at the start. Any long-term pastor or church leader can look back and see things they wish they had done differently, and, in the midst of our rapidly changing world, we would be foolish to try to plant nineteenth-century churches. So if you could start from scratch and do everything differently, what would that look like?

There is a wide range of new models for the churches we are planting, and no model is better than the others. Each must be matched to the situation, and you may need to create an entirely new response to your community's needs. These models are offered only to stimulate your thoughts; much more information is available on each of them.

Multi-Site

The multi-site approach is taken by a number of large urban churches. In its simplest form, the early service is offered on one side of town with Christian education to follow, and the later service is offered across town following their education program. The worship team simply commutes, and essentially the same service is offered in two locations. Staffing and programming may be centralized or divided between the two sites if the church owns two properties.

Some mega-churches operate multiple sites with simultaneous services. Staff may rotate, or the sermon may be presented via video or even a satellite downlink. Generally, worship is live, and only the sermon is not. This approach has been criticized greatly by mainline leaders and scholars. The ego-driven approach to ministry certainly deserves our disdain. However, there still may be something in this from which we might learn. Frankly, truly gifted preachers are rare, and often those who have that gift lack many other critical ones. If a church does have gifted preachers or teachers, why not let them do what they do well and appreciate the gifts of other leaders and pastors with equal importance and value? The world has changed, and contemporary people are quite accustomed to listening to speakers or watching live concerts on large video screens. While those of us over fifty may find this experience passive and cold, that is not true for people who grew up dancing to music on video and seeing every major event of their lives on TV.

Consider it from this perspective: given our current model for church, the limiting factor is not need, but the availability of competent clergy. There are millions of passionate, effective, devoted church leaders who have not had an opportunity to attend seminary. If we can find creative ways to empower them to plant churches and supplement what they might not know with specialists, there is no limit to the number of churches a church can establish. The bottom line is that we must consider that God may be working in new ways.

With new technology, regional airlines with inexpensive flights, and our shrinking planet, it is possible for churches to multiply new congregations at great distances. The Cathedral of Hope UCC formed a new congregation 210 miles away in another state, and another 300 miles away in a major metropolitan area. Bulletins were produced in Dallas and then transmitted electronically and printed in another city. Music was transmitted using MP3 files. The preacher flew thirty minutes to the other cities and led worship, while the congregation took responsibility for being the church. The result was the formation of churches that were not dependent upon or centered on a pastor. Circuit riders planted congregations in underserved regions two centuries ago. Perhaps we should think of places where progressive and inclusive values are not well represented and form new congregations there. If it had to be a self-generating congregation the cost would be tremendous, but an existing church can add an additional service in another city with relatively little cost and with much greater and more expedient results.

Multi-Service

A variation on the multi-site church is to consider the new plant as one more service that your church offers each week. This may be an afternoon service, offered in your current building, in which the predominant language is Spanish. It might be an evening service offered in another community using some of the same staff or volunteers that led worship in the morning. These services may be similar or radically different from the main service. Since the new plant is smaller, the services often are more casual, or, if the new plant is younger, the worship style may be more contemporary.

Beyond Sunday service, other programs likely would be based in the new location and other activities and ministries centered in that community. The staff of the church being born is actually employed by the "mother" congregation. The idea is that this site eventually will become a wholly independent congregation. At that point, they likely would employ their own pastor, but they may continue to share some staff with the originating church.

House Churches

House churches are a healthy way to get started, though some models propose this as the ultimate expression of how churches should be organized. For mainline purposes, it is probably a good way to think about how to create a solid core group with which to begin. Following the classic cell-group model, you would train four to eight people as small group leaders, allowing every small group to have a leader and an apprentice. The idea is for people to invite folks to attend their small group meeting with them and, thus, get connected. As a group grows, it soon will outgrow the living room of the host. The group then multiplies (never divides) into two small groups. The apprentice leads the second one, and the process begins again. When a community has four to eight such small groups, gathering them for worship is easy, and a core group is established with a program of community, Christian education, and even pastoral care in place.

With this kind of small group community the leadership of the founding church can work with and through the small group leaders to meet the needs of the community. Effectively done, each small group cares for one another, learns together, and tackles service projects together. The leaders become the heroes/VIPs of the community. There is little that can kill a church that has a foundation of strong small groups led by effectively trained and well-coached leaders.

Emergent Churches

Let me acknowledge from the outset that this model is a misuse of one of the ideas and values at the core of the emergent church movement. The idea that we would treat the emergent movement as a methodology or a target outcome would be abhorrent to proponents of the emerging church. However, it is a fact that mainline churches have very effectively and deliberately given birth to emergent churches.

A movement that began in the early 1990s outside the United States, the emergent church is difficult to define because of its diversity. Eddie Gibbs and Ryan Bolger, in their book *Emerging Churches: Creating Christian Community in Postmodern Cultures,* define emerging in this way:

> Emerging churches are communities that practice the way of Jesus within postmodern cultures. This definition encompasses nine practices. Emerging churches (1) identify with the life of Jesus, (2) transform the secular realm, and (3) live highly communal lives. Because of these three activities, they (4) welcome the stranger, (5) serve with generosity, (6) participate as producers, (7) create as created beings, (8) lead as a body, and (9) take part in spiritual activities.

Still unclear what the emergent church is? You are not alone. That may be the result of the fact that we are still in the midst of it. The emerging, or emergent, church movement takes its name from the idea that, as culture changes, a new church should emerge in response. In this case, it is a response by various church leaders to the current era of postmodernism. The question is what will your church's response be? Can you give life to something that is more movement than institution? Can you allow worship styles and practices to emerge from the consensus of the people gathered? Does dialogue have a place in worship, or should it in order to be didactic? Is experiential and transformational worship too risky in your setting? Would your congregation be willing to form a congregation that is radically different from the "mother" church?

Radically Inclusive

We all agree that the Dominion of God is not segregated; thus, the ideal is that the church would not be either. Still, this ideal is rarely lived out. Hispanic folks grew up in Catholic churches and find Gospel music uncomfortable; African-Americans are unlikely to attend a church where the pastor is a lesbian; affluent folks want to attend a church where there are children, and most street people don't have children who accompany them to church; emergent folk become very uncomfortable when the schizophrenic take over the conversational sermon every week. These are offensive stereotypes, of course, but they do hint at some of the challenges we face as we seek to live into our value of being a radically inclusive church.

When our hospitality seeks to move beyond tolerance, a multitude of issues arise that require deep commitment, profound trust, and hard work. Unfortunately, newly formed and forming communities have not had time to create a culture of genuine trust, and the commitment to the community is new and tender. Hence, creating a multi-ethnic/multi-cultural/multi-racial church from the start is a noble goal that is seldom realized.

What is more realistic, perhaps, is to gather all comers around a value of radical hospitality. If all agree that the new body should be genuinely welcoming of all, then the foundation is set for what may someday be an authentically diverse community. This requires foundational work with the leaders and the founding core. It also requires an ongoing system of education, training, and sensitization. It is critical that visible leadership look like those we are seeking to welcome if a church wishes to welcome those who are different from the majority.

A church that practices radical hospitality synchronizes every part of its program and ministry to reinforce that value. Everything, from the campus to child care to worship is evaluated through the experience of the first-time guest. The membership understands its role as hosts and its orientation to be servants. The songs sung must be free of even subtly racist imagery. Illustrations must include nontraditional couples and families. Holidays such as Juneteenth, Cinco de Mayo, and Gay Pride must be celebrated, even though they are secular. Everyone must feel they have a place at the table that was set before they arrived.

It should be no surprise that our highest goal is also our toughest one. Growth is slow in a place that celebrates differences.

Conflicts are frequent. Success, when it finally comes, is a taste of heaven on earth, though the participants may never fully know it in this life.

Targeted Plants

Simply put, the targeted plants model is an attempt to develop a congregation that will serve an underserved people. Logically, it will be more successful if the new congregation is similar in makeup to the birthing congregation. Not having to create or locate new resources is a major savings. Still, in denominations that are so majorly white and heterosexual, we cannot rely on lesbian, gay, bisexual, and transgender (LGBT) churches to reach LGBT people, or African-American churches to form new African-American congregations, or Hispanic churches to minister to the fastest-growing segment of the population.

Just as society discovered that affirmative action was required if our goal of equality was to be achieved, so too the mainline must work proactively if historically underrepresented populations are to have a place at the table. While the ideal may be a church that genuinely includes all people, we live in a world where that is not the case, and, as a result, faith communities serving minorities are critically important.

- People of color who must work all week with a majority of white people, and for white people, need churches where their own stories are told, and their struggles acknowledged, and their victories celebrated. Justice requires us to plant churches that will serve people still victimized by racism.

- Only a handful of states recognize the relationships of LGBT people as legal, and even fewer churches honor them as sacred. Even if we belong to one of those few denominations, we must recognize still that gay and lesbian couples live their lives out in atmospheres of derision and repression. To gather on Sunday mornings without wondering if someone will be offended if you hold your partner's hand is life-giving. To spend one hour of your life where you are safe and in the majority is sacred.

◆ Welcoming the stranger and making a place for the immigrant is a biblical mandate. What better way to provide hospitality than to create safe places where immigrants are the majority and where they determine for themselves what their worship experience will be? While all people should be fully welcomed in all our churches, we unfortunately live in a world where true spiritual sanctuaries are vital.

This list might be broadened to include creating communities where women who have been abused can find their voice again, where people struggling with addictions might take steps back to sobriety, where the sounds of silence reveal a community of the hearing impaired worshiping with their hands. Creating a diverse community and practicing radical hospitality must always be at the heart of who we are as a church. However, we also must acknowledge that no church can fully meet everyone's needs. Often the marginalized in our society may need the partnership of majority communities of faith in order to create spaces where they are empowered.

The kind of church you are planting must become clear at the intersection of who your church is and what the community's need is. Some churches may form a dozen of the same kinds of congregations. For others, the work may be different every time. Your job is to listen to the whisper of the Spirit and the heart cry of the people longing for God's grace.

Reclaiming our heritage as church planters is a vital key to the future of progressive churches. Also, these new churches we are multiplying should be born with an awareness that sooner rather than later they should become incubators for another new church to be born. This orientation enhances the health of a new church start in many ways.

Long-established churches may need to give life to a new congregation or new congregations on their own campus. These new churches may be attended by folks who speak a different language or have a different lifestyle. A terrible mistake established churches have made is their willingness — and sometimes desperate need — to "rent their building." The small income from that may be helpful, but, in the end, there are many headaches and little new life for the existing congregation. *Never* rent your building. Instead create covenant relationships that multiply the effectiveness and vitality of your congregation. This new relationship may bring in additional funds, but of much greater value will be the sense of mission and purpose and life that comes from the new relationship that is formed and sustained.

Churches are not in the rental business; we are in the relational business. We can form new congregations within our church, and we can adopt new congregations into our family. Either and both multiply the ministry of an existing church if we understand this as ministry rather than financial management. We are a people whose holy scripture often speaks of the elderly bringing forth life. No church is too old to multiply its effectiveness, and no church is too young to make multiplication a part of its identity.

Just as all of our communication must be designed with the possibility of viral marketing in mind, so too our churches must start every new group, ministry, and congregation with that mind-set. We never know when something will take off, but its chances are greatly enhanced if we have laid the proper groundwork to allow it to happen. We never know when or where the Spirit may blow. Our job is to keep our sails trimmed and be prepared when it happens.

A free manual for churches interested in multiplication is available through the Center for Progressive Renewal. It can be sent to you electronically by emailing *david@progressiverenewal.org*.

SEVEN

Twenty-First-Century Stewardship

by Coy D. James, Canon of Stewardship,
Cathedral of Hope UCC, Dallas

A recent Barna Group survey showed that the people most likely to give 10 percent of their income to a church or other nonprofit are evangelical Christians. Those least likely to give include atheists, agnostics, and liberals. What is that about? Are evangelicals more grateful for what they have been given than liberals? Do they love God more? Do evangelicals have greater faith in a generous God? I don't think any of that is true. However, we liberals may be more uncomfortable talking about money in church. Could it really be as simple as that? Is our timidity keeping us from realizing the dreams God has for all of us? Have we become so polite and intellectually superior that we have slipped into a lukewarm faith? Why are we so shy about teaching a fundamental spiritual discipline so clearly emphasized by the Jesus we follow? We do our congregations a disservice when we fail to teach the joy of living a generous life.

How can we overcome our nervousness when it comes to preparing the saints to live generous lives? How can we overcome the fear of appearing to act like televangelists when it comes to asking people to be generous and begin to teach, as much as Jesus did, about how to have a healthy, generous attitude toward money and possessions? Ministry doesn't happen without cost. The amount of ministry and the degree to which lives are changed — for those who receive the ministry and those who give it — are directly proportional to the amount of resources a faith community is willing to share.

Perhaps another reason why we find it difficult to raise money in a liberal church is that we may not be doing enough meaningful and effective ministry. Here is an astounding statistic: UNICEF has determined that thirty-five thousand children die every year of preventable diseases. They say that an investment of $2.5 billion, spent wisely, could eliminate these needless deaths world-wide. Two and a half billion. Wow, that's a lot of money. It sounds impossible to convince people to give that much even for a good cause — until you consider that's how much Americans spend on chewing gum every year.

I read a preacher's story the other day about a woman who received an inheritance. She went to her pastor and asked, if the church received an unexpected gift, how the money could be used. The pastor thought for a minute and said, "You know, the wallpaper in the ladies' restroom really needs to be replaced." She wrote him a $500 check to pay for the cost of the project and gave the rest of her planned $100,000 gift to a local charity that had a bigger dream for how to use the money to do real ministry in the community.

Where is the focus of ministry in your church? Is it limited to those who happen to attend, or are the people who attend trained to be ministers who do meaningful and effective ministry in the community? How would you use an extra $100,000? Once again, George Barna describes the trend: "Millions of people are shifting their allegiance to different forms of church experience, and a more participatory society is altering how they serve others. Many Christians are now investing greater amounts of their time and money in service organizations that are not associated with a church."

People who are actively involved in a ministry have a personal interest in the success of that ministry and, therefore, are more likely to support the church with their money. In their book *Simply Strategic Stuff,* authors Tim Stevens and Tony Morgan suggest that church leaders should have a strategy of planning new ministries, church-wide events, campaigns, or projects every six months just to generate and maintain momentum. That way the whole church will always be looking forward to something new even as they remember and celebrate a positive event that happened within the past few months.

You will find that very few give because the church needs the money, but you will be amazed at how generous people will be when the money is to be used to fund a big dream to do great work that benefits those in the community who need it most.

I have spent more than twenty years in ministry and leadership at the Cathedral of Hope UCC in Dallas, Texas. What I'm going to share in this chapter about stewardship comes from what I've learned from study, making plenty of mistakes, and being mentored by gifted pastors and church leaders. These are the things that have caused a church of 250 members with an annual budget of about $180,000 to grow to more than 4,000 members with an annual budget of $3 million. Believe me, if we can do it, so can you.

A Compelling Vision

Even in difficult economic times, people will give to a compelling vision or mission. I love this passage from Habakkuk:

> Write the vision on tablets so that a runner may read it. If it seems to tarry, wait for it; it will surely come, it will not delay.   —Habakkuk 2:2–3

At the Cathedral of Hope, our vision for many years has been to be a source of hope for lesbian, gay, bisexual, transgender (LGBT) and other marginalized people living in isolation. We want to change the way the world thinks about LGBT people, and we want to change the way LGBT people think about God. The name of the church is really a shorthand version of our vision. When we first articulated that vision in the late 1980s, we had no idea how we could accomplish it. This, of course, was before the Internet. The only example we had was Robert Schuller's television program, *The Hour of Power,* which is broadcast worldwide. The problem was we didn't have the $50 million he spent every year to buy airtime, so we knew that was not an option for us. Nevertheless, we believed this vision was God-given, so we were determined to allow God to work through us to make it a reality. Today, our website is visited each month by more than one hundred thousand visitors from all over the world. An average of seventy thousand people watch our television broadcast each week in North Texas. Our worship service is also broadcast on public access channels across the country. We now have national members in all fifty states and forty-one foreign countries. All this is due to the generosity of our constituents and their commitment to our vision.

Spiritual Discipline

People give when three components are present. Ongoing commitment rests on an *emotional connection* to a cause or purpose. The cause must be *credible and achievable,* based on vision, leadership, and track record. Finally, people give because they are taught to be generous and that teaching becomes integrated as one of their core *spiritual values and beliefs.* Generous living is taught at the Cathedral of Hope in every membership class, small group study, children's church, and adult education class. It's one of six spiritual covenants new members make when they take their membership vows. It is preached from the pulpit and modeled by the pastors, staff, and lay leaders.

Still, we are challenged every day to do a better job reaching out to those who haven't yet decided to financially support our ministries. It's a constant issue, and we spend a lot of effort to think of new and engaging ways to teach this basic spiritual discipline. Consider how often generosity is taught in your setting. Is it enough to cause generosity to become instilled as a core spiritual value? Billy Graham once said people go through three conversions: one of the head, one of the heart, and one of the pocketbook. It's true. You can tell what god people serve by reading their checkbook register.

Leadership Commitment

You will have the credibility to ask others to live generously only when you are committed personally to being generous and determined to model generosity as a leader. That also goes for your staff leadership team and governing body. I have tried in the past to make tithing a requirement of leadership, particularly for the governing body. In my view, you can be an effective manager of the sacrificial tithes and offerings of a congregation only when you give sacrificially yourself. Leaders who have the responsibility of managing the church budget must have the spiritual maturity of a generous giver before they can direct the gifts of others in a visionary way. In reference to the church budget, or what we refer to as "Goals for Ministry," Rev. Piazza has a great saying: "We can either lower the river or raise the bridge."

Boards of directors — or whatever you call your governing body — are pretty good at lowering the river (cutting expenses) but they are usually less skilled at raising the bridge (raising the money necessary to fund ministry). If members of your governing body can tell you exactly how much the church electric bill is each month, but have no idea how much the church is spending or should be spending on ministry, there is a real spiritual focus problem. An investment in leadership training and development in this area can reap amazing benefits for ministry.

We also have worked to equip people within the congregation who do give to respond when their friends or family make comments like, "All they talk about is money!" The response should be, "Actually, all they talk about is ministry. The more money we give the more ministry we can do in our community." The ministry and mission of the church will be far more successful when everyone takes personal responsibility for funding the dreams God has for our faith community. Take the risk of dreaming big dreams. Take on ministries that seem impossible to accomplish without God's help. If we have learned anything at the Cathedral of Hope, it's that God is very fond of impossible dreams. Never ever, ever start a sentence with, "Well, we're just a small church, so we can't." Reread the story of Gideon and remind leaders how God works with those who are courageous in their faith and willing to take risks to achieve the vision.

Building Trust

Most fundraising professionals will tell you that fundraising really isn't about money at all. It's about building relationships, and all relationships are based on trust and mutual respect. It takes time to build trusting relationships, but the investment of time results in donors who are genuine partners and caring ministers. Having this sort of close, personal relationship is made more difficult as a church reaches three hundred or five hundred or one thousand members. It becomes impossible for a lead pastor to bear sole responsibility for this aspect of ministry, and it makes the participation of lay leaders and volunteers all the more important in this process.

A trusting relationship is essential for effective stewardship. Leadership credibility and track record for using the congregation's gifts is critical. Trust is built when there is a transparent accounting of how gifts are used and what results were achieved with those gifts. Share stories of how each ministry is impacting the community and what could be done with additional gifts. Give members the opportunity to share their ministry experiences.

Trust also is built when there are systems in place to ensure that donors receive immediate response to questions and acknowledgement of gifts. Responses to donors should happen as quickly as possible and be as personal as possible. Documented processes reviewed regularly and used to train those who participate result in increased donor confidence in your ability to solve complex problems and carry out important ministry effectively.

Basic Infrastructure

An adequate computer system, church management software, and trained staff or volunteers have become a requirement of the modern church. This doesn't have to be a huge expense, but inevitably some expense is necessary. For example, there are many great church management software products available today, but if you're just beginning to appreciate the value of a well-maintained church mailing list, you can accomplish a great deal using an Excel spreadsheet or Access database to gather information about congregants and guests.

In order to communicate with and engage your congregation and the community effectively, you need to know as much about them as possible. The ability to sort and segment your list based on certain information and characteristics is critical to successful stewardship. In addition to the basics of name, address, and phone numbers, you need to gather email addresses, birth dates, children's names, professional skills, hobbies, volunteer interests, giving history, social networking sites to which they belong, etc. All this information will allow you to tailor stewardship appeals to reach those most interested in supporting specific ministry programs. (More about this when we get to strategic planning.)

We have discovered with our congregation that hardly anyone carries cash or writes checks anymore. Any stewardship program can be far more successful if you have systems in place to accommodate those who prefer to give by credit/debit card, bank draft, or electronic check. Our "auto-giver" program has worked very well as the most convenient way to give, and it helps ensure consistent cash flow through traditionally low attendance summer months. Even when people are not able to be present, their electronic gifts ensure the ministry and mission of the church aren't interrupted because of cash flow issues. Forty percent of our budget is underwritten by auto-givers, and we work all year long to increase the number of program participants. We've also installed a giving kiosk in the narthex to allow those who prefer to give anonymously a way to do so. Once out-of-town guests dropped by on a weekday to see the "big gay church." When they noticed the giving kiosk, they were able to leave a $3,500 gift for the church they have grown to love online.

Strategic Planning

As with most churches, there is more going on at any given moment at the Cathedral of Hope than anyone would believe. We are infamous for a "ready, fire, aim" approach to project implementation. But when we do develop a plan and stick to it, we are far more successful. Even when the Spirit blows through and plays havoc with the church calendar, or drops brilliant, but last-minute, ideas on our leadership team, we can adjust more effectively when we have a carefully defined plan. The strategic planning cycle illustrated below is one tool we use to create and implement our stewardship programs.

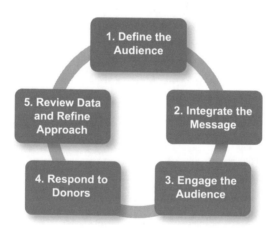

1. Define the Audience

With any stewardship appeal, it is important to match a specific message to a specific audience segment. This is where all your work to gather information about your congregants pays off. You might want to deliver different content to faithful and consistent donors, to new givers who have not signed up to be an auto-giver, or to those who give electronically, or to those who give to support specific ministries. You also might want to make message delivery decisions based on which audience segments respond to direct mail vs. email vs. appeals from friends on Facebook, Twitter, or other social networking site.

Perhaps you are making a planned giving appeal and want to make sure you communicate to all those with a certain birth date criterion. The more personal the message and the more you can demonstrate you have a personal relationship with the donor, the more likely your appeal will be successful. Doing a good job with this step also ensures a more cost-effective program.

2. Integrate the Message

A cardinal rule of marketing is that a message must be delivered successfully at least seven times before the recipient actually hears it. This is important to consider if you are relying on one stewardship sermon or sermons only as the sole source for stewardship education and motivation for the congregation.

Creating a clear, concise, and consistent message integrated into all stewardship, evangelism, communications, education, and marketing products provides the necessary repetition and brand identity to ensure that the message is heard, understood, and reinforced. Be sure not only that the content is consistent but also that all associated graphic elements, slogans, pictures, and collateral handouts match for each appeal.

3. Engage the Audience

In this step, define all the methods you are able to use to get your message to the appropriate audience. Use as many methods as you can afford, analyzing each for its cost-effectiveness and historical success. This could include a well-designed and compelling website, emails, electronic newsletters, interactive online flip-books, news stories and public relations messages for local media, Facebook, Twitter, and other social networks, in addition to printed materials, handouts, and pulpit announcements.

Every communication method should drive readers to your website for more information and to make online gifts. Take every opportunity and every occasion to collect information from donors, particularly email addresses. Dr. Schuller once said he built the Crystal Cathedral with a mailing list. It's not possible to overstate the importance of a well-maintained donor database.

Keys to success in this step include creativity, repetition, consistency of message and graphic design, interactivity, using well-prepared congregants and lay leaders, and making the presentation fun and emotionally compelling.

4. Respond to Donors

Donors demand and deserve heartfelt appreciation, considerate and responsive treatment, and information that inspires trust. In this step, develop or review a comprehensive donor response plan that includes a listing of all the ways a donor can make a contribution, who is responsible for receiving the gift, and who will write a personal acknowledgment.

It is important to review, update, and retrain participants regarding changes to the donor response plan with each new appeal. Make sure that all those who have a responsibility in this plan understands their role in the process and the importance of excellent and timely performance of their tasks. Key components of the acknowledgment note include a mention of the appeal that resulted in the gift, the fund that received the gift, and the importance of the gift to the success of the ministry. All of our notes are handwritten and are sent within the week the contribution is received. All gifts are acknowledged as quickly as possible to create a "wow" experience for the donor.

Although some fundraising professionals say you should never miss an opportunity to ask for a gift, we never solicit a new gift in an acknowledgement. We believe it affects trust and mistakenly gives the donor the impression that all we really care about is the money.

5. Review Data and Refine Approach

At the conclusion of any appeal, it is important to spend some time analyzing what worked and what didn't. Perhaps one message was more effective than another or one delivery method worked better than others. Who responded and who didn't? Is any follow-up needed with specific donors from whom you expected a contribution? What was the final cost of the appeal compared to the amount contributed? Was the cost-benefit ratio better, worse, or the same as other appeals and why? Answering all these questions and making adjustments in strategy will make the next appeal even more successful.

Other Lessons Learned

Most generous donors start with small gifts and grow their giving over time as their trust in the organization grows, confidence in the ability of leadership to achieve worthy projects increases, and their own personal involvement gives them a sense of responsibility for the success of the mission of the church. Develop a strategy for each audience segment to encourage incremental increases in giving over time.

We've learned that most people in our congregation are more likely to buy than to give. That is, they are more likely to fund specific projects like money for Katrina victims, or school supplies for children, or choir robes, or daily nutritious meals for children in Mexican border towns than to give to a general fund. Make sure you provide multiple opportunities for congregants to support ministries that motivate generous giving.

Resources

printingforless.com: When only something printed will do

theprintplace.com: Alternate cost-effective printing source

mrpostcard.com: Low-cost postcard printer

OneCallNow.com: Easy and inexpensive telephone tree with texting capability

smallthinksbig@gmavt.net: Sue Small, flipbook products design and discounted flipbook hosting *zmags.com:* Sample flipbook products, software source/host site

securegive.com: Source for onsite giving kiosk

ministrymarketingcoach.com: Great marketing "how to" resources

americanchurch.com: American Church, Inc., giving envelopes, online giving and stewardship services

ucc.org/stewardship/still-speaking-money: For online giving and credit card processing

mgive.com: Using the "texting" capability of your mobile phone to contribute to a cause

firstgiving.com: Member fundraising through social network pages

ePhilanthropy.org: Establishing online trust with the Code of Ethical Online Philanthropic Practices

ConstantContact.com: Mass email support

EIGHT

Transformational Leadership Skills

In September of 2009, I found myself on the phone with a young pastor of an urban church on the verge of closing its doors. He had been at this church for two years, and despite his best efforts to turn the church around, it had declined to an average of twelve people on Sunday mornings. He had tried everything that he could think of to grow this congregation; the congregation, likewise, had allowed him the freedom to try new ministries and programs. Nothing seemed to work.

His call to me was one of desperation. He was tired, disillusioned, and thinking of leaving the ministry. He had given this church everything he had, but nothing changed. He was convinced that he was a poor leader and that God was grieving his failure in this church. It was one of the most pain-filled conversations I have had with a church leader, one that changed my life.

I am passionate about leadership. I always have had an interest in how leaders affect change in their organizations, but after that phone call I became passionate for a different reason. I learned that good leaders may have natural talent, but they need training, coaching, and support. Excellence in leadership can be taught, and I am convinced that part of our resurrection as a denomination, and as the church of Jesus Christ, will come through each of us committing to improve our level of leadership capacity.

John Maxwell, in his well-known book *The 21 Irrefutable Laws of Leadership,* starts with the "Law of the Lid," which is simply this: Leadership ability is the lid that determines a person's level of effectiveness. The lower an individual's ability to lead, the lower the lid on her potential. The higher the leadership skills, the greater his effectiveness.

When Rev. Cindy Andrews-Looper started a Bible study in her home in Nashville, she had no idea that she actually was giving formation to a church that would have more than three hundred members within ten years. What she did understand was the Law of the Lid, and, with each new person added to the congregation, Cindy understood that her leadership capacity had to grow. She learned how to attract people, inspire them, and create space for them to share their gifts. She literally reinvented herself as a leader at each stage of her congregation's growth. Holy Trinity Community Church is noted as a fast-growing congregation in the Southeast because Cindy understands basic leadership growth.

There are hundreds of books about leadership. Many of them are very good. What we offer here are the leadership lessons that we have learned by working with pastors across the country and through our own experience. Let us be clear. We are not leadership experts. We are learning along with everyone else. Perhaps that is one way in which our leadership models are changing. Effective leaders today are no longer the experts; we are the networkers, the collaborators, the facilitators, the lifelong learners. In the past, leadership was a hierarchical position into which one ascended. Today leadership has nothing to do with titles or positions and everything to do with influence, wisdom, and the ability to collaborate. Despite the cultural changes in leadership, as John Maxwell is so fond of saying, in politics, business, or church, "Everything rises or falls on leadership."

So what is the secret to effective leadership in a twenty-first century progressive church? Maxwell offered twenty-one, but we will settle for seven:

Ready, Fire, Aim

Entrepreneurial leaders love the phrase "ready, fire, aim" because it appears to be action-oriented. Their criticism of the church is that we spend too much time discussing, debating, and planning and too little time doing. However the "ready, fire, aim" approach can be as ineffective as the style the action-oriented criticize unless you invest at least as much in the "ready" and "aim" as in the "fire."

Ready

In previous generations, it was important to persuade churches to develop strategic plans for how they intended to live into their future. This exercise was invaluable in helping churches who had done things the same way for decades (if not centuries) to consider the possibility of a different approach to fulfilling their mission. Actually, the greatest benefit might have been in challenging churches to identify what their mission and ministry were in their specific context. It helped free many institutions of complacency and presumption.

Today the rate of change can render the planning process almost impossible. By the time a community has researched the challenges and problems, clarified the objectives, identified the possible solutions, and built consensus, the whole world may have changed. In 1990, the Cathedral of Hope UCC identified as one of its missions reaching lesbian and gay people in small towns where there were no welcoming churches. At the time, the only way they knew to do this was on television. In the course of their research, they discovered that the Crystal Cathedral, under the leadership of Robert Schuller, was spending $50 million a year just to purchase airtime. That was utterly inconceivable to a church that, at the time, had fewer than five hundred members. Still, they began to move toward the only solution that was available to them. They created a fledgling television ministry incrementally. No one could have anticipated the changes in communication that would come about with the Internet. As it turned out, because of their preparations, when the Internet became available in every community, the Cathedral of Hope had the systems and equipment to broadcast its worship services on the web to more than one million people a year.

Strategic preparation has replaced strategic planning as the way in which effective leaders get a congregation ready for the opportunities to fulfill their mission in new and creative ways. In the Ready-Fire-Aim approach to leadership, a community of faith must have identified its vision, core values, and unique mission so clearly that it is able to integrate them into its very DNA. Leadership gets a church ready for the moment when the Spirit presents opportunities to live into their call. "Ready" is the process by which a congregation becomes unconsciously competent. When both the youngest and the oldest confirmed members of a church can articulate the church's unique identity and mission, you will know that your leadership has prepared them for the opportunities of the future.

Fire

Some leaders simply throw things against the wall to see what sticks. This is certainly one approach to identifying what might work. The problem, of course, is that it makes a mess of the kitchen. Trying a lot of things at once is what Michael Gerber, in his book *The E-Myth Revisited*, calls an "entrepreneurial seizure." The leaders in the church mobilize the congregation around the threat of decline and then implement barely developed programs into the church life, with no ways to measure effectiveness, impact, or strategic alignment. Put in a theological framework, leaders fail to discern the steady leading of the Spirit and lose sight of who and what God has called them to be.

If, however, the groundwork has been laid carefully, it is important for the church to try out new projects, programs, and ministries as a lab for identifying what might or might not work. These small-scale trial ministries don't often develop into much, but they can be incubators for other ideas and new leaders. You never know when one might spark a fire of renewal.

The challenge with developing an extensive and comprehensive plan before "firing" is that, by the time you discover it doesn't work, too many people are deeply invested and adjustments are difficult and sometimes divisive. If an extensively planned ministry doesn't work, it is difficult to declare it dead and move on. Often valuable time and resources are wasted, and when it is finally laid to rest, the entire community feels like a failure. If, however, small ventures had been attempted along the way, much could have been learned. Creating opportunities for failure is major preparation for success. Jesus noted how often God sent prophets who apparently were ignored, but in retrospect we know that they prepared the way for the redeeming work of God in Christ.

Mainline denominations have been notorious for spending millions of dollars developing copious plans and rolling them out with great fanfare, only to discover they were not what the congregations needed or wanted. So too mainline congregations often make plans based on the reality of their closed community. New people and young people who have limited spare time, and an even shorter supply of ecclesiastical patience, find endless committee meetings and planning sessions to be a poor investment of their time. They are likely to go down the road to the Salvation Army, whose theology they may find untenable, but the Salvation Army knows its mission and will put them to work.

Aim

Churches are notoriously bad at evaluation. People tend to own programs or ministries and no one comes near them. The church still meets at 11:00 on Sunday mornings because people need time to feed and milk the cows, then bathe, dress, and take the wagon to town to go to church. Perhaps it is time to consider a service for members who don't raise cows, but this is one of a myriad of practices the church still hasn't had the courage to examine.

When a new person comes into the church with a burning desire to answer what they believe to be God's call, a dying church will assign this person to a committee. A vibrant church will be able to measure, almost instantly, the value of the idea because they know who they are and what their mission is. If the idea is congruent with the congregation's mission, values, and identity, a healthy response would be to ask the person to put together a team of folks and help them experiment on a limited scale to "test the call." If the results are positive, then a more comprehensive plan can be developed

Having recently survived teaching teenagers to drive, I can see an obvious illustration of this principle. Teaching them the rules of the road, how the vehicle works, and how to find their way around a complex city was just the beginning of getting them ready to take to the road. Ultimately, it was practice that was most needed so that they could do a dozen things at once and still make split-second decisions. Their instinctive reactions would determine if they would be safe drivers. As is often the case, their first accident came soon after they got their licenses. It was the result of underdeveloped reactions. Driving skills come only from practice, and, likewise, trying to aim a program without trying it out is as irrational as driving a car at sixty-five miles an hour during rush hour without having practiced first on empty roads. Comprehensive planning is almost impossible in the dynamic and changing environment in which our churches must live today.

Having said that, though, we should note that the failing of many churches is found in their unwillingness to evaluate. This often means telling someone the truth in love, and we risk their being offended. As a result, we continue ministries long after their effectiveness has ended. The cost is that we are unwilling to start new programs or to attempt new strategies. The church is held captive by its cowardice when "the truth would set them free." An effective leader knows what success would look like and builds into every new program, ministry, and mission a time and way to evaluate it. As trite as it may seem, effective leaders are responsible for reminding everyone that, as Thomas Edison learned, success often is discovering what doesn't work.

You Cannot Lead What You Do Not Live

To say that another way: You cannot teach what you have not learned, and you cannot lead where you have not been. The movie *Invictus,* starring Matt Damon and Morgan Freeman, tells the story of how South African president Nelson Mandela motivated his country's rugby team, the Springboks, to victory in the 1995 World Cup competition. Recognizing his country's desperate need for reconciliation and hope for a brighter future, Mandela chose their losing, ragged rugby team as his best hope for uniting the white Africanas and the black South Africans. Both loved the sport of rugby.

Mandela invited the young white captain of the team to his office one afternoon. As he was serving tea, Mandela said, "Tell me Francois, how do you inspire your team to do their best?"

Francois replied "By example. I have always thought you lead by example, sir."

"Well, that is right. That is exactly right. But how to get them to be better than they think they can be? That is very difficult, I find."

Mandela left Francois without the answer to his question, but he knew the answer would come. It was the question that was most important. How do we get our leaders, our churches, to be better than they think they can be?

It starts with us, and it flows from there.

Becoming a leader is not an event; it is a process. Nelson Mandela was able to lead his country and inspire the wider world because he unjustly spent thirty years in a jail cell and chose to learn the power of forgiveness and the strength of the human spirit. Who he genuinely was found expression in his leadership. His life made his leadership so powerful. He lived what he led. Sooner or later, we all do.

When we take the name "Christian," you and I are given the privilege of modeling a Christ-like life for the world. We make the claim that, through the power of the Holy Spirit and God's word to us, we are a transformed people; we are the resurrected Body of Christ. Yet in too many of our congregations, transformation is the last thing that visitors might experience on a Sunday morning. More than likely, they will experience subdued worship, slightly unfamiliar music, an odd smelling building, and people who all but ignore their presence. Visitors must wonder just what this redemption/transformation is all about if we are its models.

Leaders in our churches today must have the ability to live what they lead. More directly put, we have to walk the walk *and* talk the talk. If we make the claim that God's love can transform the world, we also should be able to talk about and show how it has transformed us as individuals. If you make the claim that you can find new life in Christ, we should live and lead in such a way that people can see that claim at work in us. It takes time, discipline, and sacrifice to truly integrate the values we claim.

As the Springbok captain illustrated, great leaders lead by example. They show up, pay attention, and participate directly in getting amazing things done. They show by the way live their daily lives that they are committed to the values they espouse. Through their lives and their examples, they inspire others to greatness.

It is also true that, in a postmodern world, it is crucial that leaders be vulnerable and authentic, willing to reveal that they are struggling with the same issues as their fellow pilgrims. No longer is the church the place where the most educated person in town is employed. Pastors and other church leaders must not pretend to know the answers to questions too profound or painful to articulate. Often, our leadership must be modeled by our faith, despite our doubts, and by our faithfulness without having all the answers. While we do not need to use the pulpit or congregation to work through our own issues, it is important that we model our willingness to live with life's questions. The last thing our churches need is another expression of artificial certainty. If they want leadership that knows the answers and is willing to call them to conformity, there are probably several fundamentalist churches in town they could attend.

Perfection is not the value that is needed of modern leaders; integrity is. Have you integrated your faith into your life in a way that is helpful and liberating?

Ultimately, leadership is influence. The only people with any influence in our lives are people we trust. Trust is earned by being trustworthy. When it is lost, regaining it is incredibly hard. It is your greatest asset. Don't squander it, and don't lose it. Give people a reason to trust you, and your leadership will spring from the core of who you are, not from your position. Leading from position is the weakest leadership of all.

Leaders Make Leaders

In our celebrity-obsessed culture, we may be tempted to equate leaders with organizational stars. This leads us to expectations and behaviors that make us the center of attention in every group or event. Oh, we all give lip service to that idea: "When a project is completed by a good leader people say 'Look what she did.' When a project is completed by a great leader people say, 'Look what we did.'" That sounds good, but often it is not reflected in how we lead. The very best leaders are invisible because they have recruited, trained, coached, and supported others to be the visible leaders. This should be particularly true for pastors whose biblical mandate is to "equip the people for the work of ministry." Our principal equipping role must be to develop the leadership gifts of others.

The good news is that if you do this the right way, you end up making life infinitely easier for yourself. Good leaders raise up more good leaders in their organizations.

Here is what this looks like: For too many of us, cultivating new leaders in our churches is an accidental process. I ask you, at this moment, who are you cultivating into ministry? Who are you mentoring in Christian service? If you focus your time in developing the leaders of your church rather than followers — leaders who then cultivate more leaders — you will experience exponential growth. This is how we grow churches: by growing leaders.

Jim Collins wrote an important book in 2001 called *Good to Great*. In it he and his research team studied why some companies become great institutions, and why others plateau or fail. He discovered that in every success the organization was headed by a Level 5 leader. Level 5 leaders, he writes, "channel their ego needs away from themselves and into the larger goal of building a great company. It's not that Level 5 leaders have no ego or self-interest. Indeed, they are incredibly ambitious — but their ambition is first and foremost for the institution, not themselves." Level 5 leaders are leaders who attract, equip, and empower leaders around them.

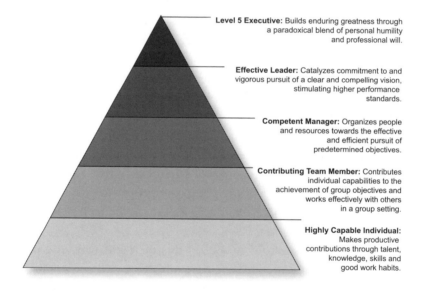

Leadership Levels by Jim Collins

What makes this kind of leadership so powerful is a delicate balance between humility and personal will. Great leaders want what is best for the whole and work sacrificially to that end. In the Christian church, the pyramid probably should be inverted because Jesus said that we who are to be the greatest must be the servants of all (Matt. 20:26).

We need more Level 5 leaders who have the humility to work for the greater good and the ambition to make the church something truly great. We need leaders who can cast vision, inspire people, and mobilize them to accomplish the impossible. We need leaders who will empower others to lead. Motivational speaker Zig Ziglar is fond of saying, "There is no limit to what you can accomplish if you don't care who gets the credit."

Great leaders learn to recognize the leadership gifts of others. They discover that CEOs often can be terrible leaders, but a widowed grandmother can change the world. Recruiting, training, and coaching leaders often take more time and effort than simply doing it yourself. However, it is the difference between spending time (doing it yourself) and investing time (empowering others). When something is spent it is gone, but investments will pay off greatly in the long run.

Keeping the Main Thing

This fourth secret probably should be number one, because it is the leader's number one responsibility. As a new pastor, my first task always was to facilitate the congregation in identifying and articulating their vision — their understanding of who God is calling them to be and what God is calling them to do. This can be as simple as asking and listening in such a way that everyone has a chance to be heard. The church leadership's role is to assemble the information that has been gathered into a comprehensive and comprehensible vision.

It is critical that the vision comes from the heart of a congregation and not from staff, external consultants, or an artificial program. The leader's responsibility is to elicit the vision and then to put it into a form that can be heard, envisioned, felt deeply. Then repeat it again and again. In *Power Surge* (which is *much* better than the title or cover would indicate) Michael Foss tells a story from czarist Russia about a priest who was walking along minding his own business when a royal guard stopped him at gunpoint. The guard demanded, "What is your name? Why are you here? Where are you going?"

The priest gazed quizzically at the solder and then asked, "How much do they pay you to do this work?"

The soldier, somewhat taken aback, replied, "Why, three kopeks a month."

"I'll pay you thirty kopeks a month if you will stop me every week and ask me those same questions," the priests said.

The role of a leader is to keep lifting up those three questions:

- What does the name of this church mean in the community? What should it mean? How can we give it more meaning?

- Why are we here? Why are we still here? Why are we needed here?

- Where are we going? What is next? What should we be doing to live out our identity and calling in *this* day and age?

The leader's principal job is to call the congregation continuously to remember and renew their mission, purpose, and vision. Leaders help the community keep its agenda focused. There are many good and wonderful things that a church could do. The leader helps the community recall what it should do because of who it is uniquely called to be.

Effective leaders help us keep the main thing as the main thing. The difficult part of that may be saying, "No" to the good in order to have the resources to say, "Yes" to the best. Every other day a new program or book (like this one) comes out with some really good ideas. You must discern which ideas are for you and your congregation. You also must help others recognize which things must be released. One of the greatest challenges of our job as consultants for renewal is to get a congregation to evaluate ruthlessly all the things they are doing and to stop doing most of them. Often dying churches have more committees than they do members. We must read John chapter 15 again and again until, at last, we see pruning as a work of the Spirit. Helping good people say, "No" to worthy things so that they can say, "Yes" is one of leadership's greatest challenges and most important functions.

Leaders Give Permission

We both began our ministries very young and worked our way through college and seminary as pastors. One of the shocking discoveries for every young pastor is the amount of power people give you. While the governance of the church may be congregational, time and again, heads turn toward the pastor to ensure that the course is the right one. People often have asked my opinion about matters I knew little or nothing about. At first this puzzled and even frightened me. Eventually, I came to realize that, nine times out of ten, they already knew the right answers. What they really sought was affirmation, encouragement, and support.

Leaders don't give permission because they have the power to say yes or no. We give permission because we have influence and people will go forth with more resolve and confidence if they believe we are with them. In *Behold I Do a New Thing*, Kirk Hadaway has the courage to quote Rick Warren and talk about the positive examples from his ministry at Saddleback Community Church. Although it is a huge church with hundreds of staff members, Warren insists the staff never starts new ministries. They might suggest an idea, but they always wait until the right person steps forward to lead it. Hadaway goes on to quote from Rick Warren's *The Purpose Driven Church*:

> Expect the best of your people and trust them with ministry. Many people are so afraid of *wildfire* that they spend all their time putting out every little campfire that'll warm up the church! If you're the pastor, let others make some of the mistakes! Don't insist on making them all yourself. You bring out the best in people by giving them a *challenge*, giving them *control*, and giving them *credit*.

Amen! Despite our disagreements with Warren on other issues, on this one he is exactly on target. It is what effective leaders do! In many settings, the job of leadership is to give permission so effectively that the congregation understands that they are the people of God and don't require the permission of the pastor or a committee to take on the ministry of the Body of Christ. The first time you discover that your church is doing a ministry that you knew nothing about you will know you are a good leader. If the ministry is congruent with the vision and mission of the church, then you are a great leader.

Effective leaders do their foundational work so well that they don't need to be present when decisions are made. Leadership is not about control or decision making. Use your influence in the right ways and in the right places, and the decisions that are made will be good and right and won't need to be made by you.

Servant Leadership

Robert Greenleaf is credited with the modern understanding of servant leadership. It became widely popular after he wrote an essay and then a book entitled *Servant as Leader*. According to his essay, Greenleaf's philosophy was inspired by reading a work of fiction in 1958:

> The idea of the servant as leader came out of reading Hermann Hesse's *Journey to the East*. In this story, we see a band of men on a mythical journey.... The central figure of the story is Leo, who accompanies the party as the servant who does their menial chores, but who also sustains them with his spirit and his song. He is a person of extraordinary presence. All goes well until Leo disappears. Then the group falls into disarray and the journey is abandoned. They cannot make it without the servant Leo. The narrator, one of the party, after some years of wandering finds Leo and is taken into the Order that had sponsored the journey. There he discovers that Leo, whom he had known

first as servant, was in fact the titular head of the Order, its guiding spirit, a great and noble leader.

It was Jesus who taught us that, if we are to lead, we must be servants, but Greenleaf's work was an important reminder that had great influence on how leadership is understood by much of business and industry today. It is ironic that churches and pastors also need this reminder.

A framework helpful for understanding servant-leadership is found in the "Ten Characteristics of the Servant-Leader" described by Larry Spears in his book *Reflections on Leadership*. Spears describes ten characteristics of servant leadership:

- Listening, as opposed to our skill of always speaking. Really hearing a community's vision is the first step in effective vision casting, but it often gets missed in a community trained to listen to their leaders rather than being listened to by their leaders.

- Empathy, which is related to listening. Leaders are not listening for facts, but for feelings, hopes, needs, desires, etc.

- Healing. The role of an effective servant leader is not to impose healing from the outside but to remove the impediments so that the Body might heal naturally.

- Awareness. This begins with self-awareness, since those who lack it are rarely able to truly be present for others.

- Persuasion is offered as a contrast to leadership by the power that comes from one's position.

- Conceptualization helps groups to assemble the various pieces into a coherent vision.

- Foresight is the ability to foresee outcomes, needs, and developments. While pastors seldom live into their role as prophet today, we are offered the opportunity to read and study and observe as part of our job. In turn, we have a responsibility to use the knowledge we gain to help a community anticipate the future.

+ Stewardship. Peter Block's book *Stewardship* defines for businesses the idea of stewardship as "holding something in trust for another." Greenleaf saw the role of leaders, CEOs, staffs, trustees as holding their institutions in trust for the greater good of society. How much more true is that of church leaders?

+ Commitment to the growth of people.

+ Building community.

These characteristics are not simply traits or skills possessed by the leader; this list is an approach to our role as leaders that honors those we lead because they are those we seek to serve. Greenleaf said that servant-leadership is "an ethical perspective on leadership that identifies key moral behaviors that leaders must continuously demonstrate in order to make progress."

Servant leadership is very much akin to what Graham Standish calls "humble leadership." In his book *Becoming a Blessed Church: Forming a Church of Spiritual Purpose, Presence, and Power,* he concludes:

When we become more open to God as leaders, we are freed to find creative ways to lead people more fruitfully to God. Humble leaders try to ground their leadership in openness to God, aware of how easy it is to close ourselves to God and to lead out of fear, willfulness, cynicism, selfishness, pride, and a sense of our own power. Leading from radical openness allows us to lead by following God's lead. And this way makes all the difference between leading a congregation to regard God as an idea or thought, and leading a congregation to a spiritual place where God is encountered and experienced.

Leaders Are Courageous

I love these quotes, which, I think, speak volumes about leadership:

- "I take lots of chances but leave nothing to chance."
  — Charles Lindbergh

- "I missed *every* shot I didn't take." — Wayne Gretzky

- "I've missed more than nine thousand shots in my career. I've lost almost three hundred games. Twenty-six times I've been trusted to take the game-winning shot and missed. I've failed over and over and over again in my life. And *that* is why I succeed." — Michael Jordan

The point, of course, is that leaders have the courage to try and fail. So often when dealing with mainline leaders I want to repeat the story of the four lepers in 2 Kings 7:3. There was a famine, and, as they sat outside the city gates where they had been exiled, it became apparent that when the healthy had no food, there was none to spare for those whose only option was to beg. Eventually, one leper asked, "Why are we simply siting here until we die. Let's do *something*."

It is a leadership myth that we have to have a clear sense of the destination before we set out on the journey. Most of us think that we have to see the Promised Land clearly before we make any changes to our churches or set out on a new mission. Here is my truth: If I had waited until I clearly saw the outcome of my ministry, with every detail determined, I would still be sitting, staring at a blank computer screen. I bet the same is true for you.

In her bestselling book *Jesus, CEO*, Laurie Beth Jones quotes her mother, who once told her, "Honey, even if you're going to fall, you can always fall forward." Leadership does not come with detail-filled, certified maps, only a general sense of direction. That certainly has been my experience.

The Center for Progressive Renewal started in January 2010, and we can tell you honestly that we have no idea what this organization will look like in five years. We can't see into the future, but we are clear that why we exist: to renew the progressive church. We also are clear about how we can do that: by starting new churches and renewing existing churches.

However, we don't know where that is going to take us. Will that mean that we will strengthen existing denominations? I don't know. Will that mean we shepherd the formation of a network of progressive churches from a number of different ecumenical circles? We don't know. However, if we waited until we were clear about those questions, we wouldn't be writing this book today.

What we *have* learned on this journey is that fear is our greatest stumbling block. It is the most destructive force hindering God's redemptive work in the world. So many of the pastors with whom I work are afraid to set out on a course for fear that they will drive the ship into the ground. I say this with no judgment; I have been there myself. Instead of experimenting and playing with church, we prop up our programs long after they have served their purposes.

A compelling "why" can overcome any "how." Effective leaders know the *why* and are therefore willing to take chances and keep trying until they discover the *how*.

There are, of course, many more secrets to developing our skills as effective leaders. Let us leave you in this chapter with two final aphorisms that we find important to remember:

> If you keep doing what you have always done,
> you will keep getting what you have always gotten.

> *and*

> When the horse is dead, dismount.

It might not be a bad idea to chisel these messages on the front of every denominational headquarters in America, and many of our churches could stand to learn that lesson as well.

If we are to be effective leaders, we must be lifelong learners, for learning new self-insights, new skills, and new ways of doing things is critical for us all. Maybe the first person we must learn to lead is the person who looks out at us in the mirror each morning.

NINE

Transformational Mission

In the Bible people often asked what they needed to do to be saved. Their concern was that their life might not have eternal value. Today people seem to be more concerned about other things.

"What must I do to be happy?" he asked.

I suggested that he might try embezzling if it was a lack of money that was making him unhappy. If his marriage was the problem, infidelity might be the solution. If his life was too painful, my suggestion was drugs or alcohol to numb the pain. After about my fourth outlandish suggestion, my counselee began to catch on. Then I said, "I think happiness is the wrong goal for the human life. In my experience, happiness is really just the byproduct of a life well lived."

The corollary to that in church leadership might be that a *healthy growing church is the byproduct of a powerful externally focused mission.* It is my conviction that if we can turn our churches inside out, we would give life to another great spiritual awakening. As churches decline, they inevitably seem to fall into a pattern of drawing inward, spending more and more of their energy and resources on management and self-care. That pattern only accelerates the rate of decline, and decline seems to accelerate the need for control and self-care. Churches too often become little more than spiritual clubs whose principal mission is to meet the needs of their own members. Churches that act like a family or social group produce and manage community but little else.

So what is the secret to having a mission that can lead a church to health and vitality?

The Mission Must Be Powerful Enough to Give Meaning to Members' Lives

Progressive Christians sometimes hold Rick Warren and his *Purpose Driven Life,* in disdain and thus miss the reason that the book has sold more than 30 million copies. People are desperately looking for a way to give their lives meaning. They are looking for an answer to why they are here. Helping them discover that is the responsibility of the church, but we cannot do it merely by giving them a way to serve themselves by serving their own church.

If a church offers people an opportunity to be transformed and to become transformers, they will find purpose in their lives. As they thrive, so will the church. Jesus called us to be the salt *of the earth,* not to season our own lives. He called us to be the light *of the world,* not to settle for being personally enlightened. Some people have been attending Sunday school for decades. When will we ever graduate, and to what will we graduate? Mark Trotter, former pastor of the First United Methodist Church in San Diego, said it beautifully:

> All of us need a purpose that is large enough to include God and long enough to include eternity. We need a purpose that makes life worth living and gives meaning to our dying. We need a purpose that calls forth our true stature and elicits the hidden fire within us. As Christians, we are called to live with imagination and courage because we have a purpose that endures past sunset.

The church must become the place where people can find a purpose for their lives that is greater than earning enough money to be able to save for retirement so we can die in comfort. Only the church can give people a "purpose that endures past sunset." The mission of the church must be the tool for doing that. No one needs another excuse or occasion for self-service. What people need is for the church to offer them proof that their lives can be larger than the shrink-wrapped packaging of self-absorption.

The Church Must Change Its Own Definition of Success and Health

In order to do that, though, the church must change its own definition of success and health. C. Kirk Hadaway's book *Behold I Do a New Thing: Transforming Communities of Faith* is excellent (which means I agreed with about half of it). In it he talks about the problem of goal displacement:

> Life within the organization becomes more of a concern to the group members than the group's relationship with the outside world. What occurs is called goal displacement — a process by which the primary mission of an organization is replaced by operative goals that have little, if anything to do with the organization's original reason for being. In almost all cases, the new goals involve a focus on group maintenance and member satisfaction — particularly involving the satisfaction of a group of leaders and core members.

This describes the dynamic that guides the daily life in many of our churches. What they need is a compelling external mission to serve the needs of others. Every week they gather for worship, but then they must scatter to serve. At the end of every Sunday service, I pronounce the same benediction: "Our worship has ended, but *now* our service begins. Go from this place. You are the Body of Christ, so the whole world awaits you....." While we might use different words, when worship energizes people for service the church has found a rhythm as healthy as breathing in and then breathing out.

In his book *Missional Renaissance*, Reggie McNeal talks about the scorecards most churches use to know if they are succeeding or not: how many, how often, how much? McNeal, a missional leadership specialist for Leadership Network, wonders what a different world we could create if the score churches kept was something like:

- Number of people reporting improved marriages
- Number of people reporting increased or improved friendships
- Number of people serving other people in some venue
- Number of people being mentored
- Number of people mentoring
- Number of people able to articulate their life's mission
- Number of people reporting addiction recovery progress.

W. David Phillips made a different list on his blog. These were some of the ways he suggested we should "Measure Success in Ministry":

- Number of cigarette butts in the church parking lot
- Number of adoptions people in the church have made from local foster care
- Number of pictures on the church wall of unwed mothers holding their babies in their arms for the first time
- Number of classes for special needs children and adults
- Number of former convicted felons serving in the church
- Number of phone calls from community leaders seeking the church's advice
- Amount of money the local school has saved because of services the church has provided.

To those two lists I would add:

- Number of people who thought they'd never find a welcoming church home but now worship regularly
- Number of people recycling and using fair trade products
- Number of people who measure their net worth by what they give rather than what they have in the bank

- Number of people who have relationships with people of a different race, socio-economic class, nationality, or sexual orientation

- Number of weddings and funerals the church does that other churches won't do.

So, how does your church measure excellence? How do you know if you are succeeding or failing in fulfilling the mission Christ has for your congregation? What is your congregation's scorecard? What should it be?

The Ultimate Measure of Our Mission Must Be Jesus and How Our Mission Aligns with His

A mission that transforms the church must be a mission that transforms the world. We are, after all, called to be the risen Body of Christ. Our mission must be his mission. Jesus did not measure his life by how big his numbers were; he invested his life mostly in a small number of people who could multiply the impact of his ministry. His standard was not how much salt he could accumulate in the saltshaker or how bright the light was under a bushel basket, but rather how much of the world he could season and enlighten.

In the 1990s, the question "What would Jesus do?" (WWJD) became ubiquitous in evangelical circles. It was the revival of a phenomenon initiated by a Congregational minister named Charles Sheldon, who wrote a book published in 1896 entitled *In His Steps*. A fictional congregation is challenged to live their lives by the principle of what Jesus would or would not do. The simple question changed individuals, the church, and the community as the answer was applied with integrity. While most of us are familiar with the book, you may not know that it originated as a Sunday night sermon series at Central Congregational Church in Topeka, Kansas. It was delivered to standing-room-only crowds of young people who, then as now, desperately sought guidance about how to give their lives meaning.

Telling a story in weekly installments instead of delivering a sermon every Sunday night was a cutting edge approach to ministry at the turn of the nineteenth century. Far from the individualistic piety that accompanied the revival of the idea in the 1990s, Sheldon was a leader of the Social Gospel movement and was seeking a creative way to motivate his congregation to be involved in transformational mission. He was a strong advocate for the poor and for equality, and was a leader in racially integrating the church and in advocating women's suffrage.

In Charles Sheldon's mind, what Jesus would do, and did, was change the world. Should the mission of the local church be anything less than that today?

An Effective Mission Should Be So Great That It Requires Every Member to Be a Minister

We all probably have used the illustration of how the church is often like a football game: thousands of people needing exercise, vigorously cheer on exhausted professionals who need a rest. Of course, the church professionals largely are the ones responsible for setting up this system in which they are the ones paid to do the ministry. In a vocation where criticism is abundant and freely given, it is not surprising that we devised systems in which we could be seen as heroes who save the day and, if given half a chance, would save the world.

It is popular to say that "every member is a minister," and many churches hold this up as one of their core values in the congregational system. In reality, though, most of the ministry of the church gets done by people giving money to pay someone to do it. In his book *Power Surge*, Michael W. Foss describes the need for the church to shift the pastor's role from chaplain to leader. He writes, "Pastors must become spiritual catalysts through whom the Holy Spirit encourages, equips, directs, and strengthens the faith of those who serve." As the Apostle Paul puts it, the role of the pastor is to "equip the saints for the work of ministry" (Eph. 4:12). Not to do the work of ministry. Clergy never should be called "ministers" or should use the term only as a title shared by the entire community of faith.

Ultimately, the mission of the church should be large enough and compelling enough to draw people together, overcome divisions, and create a bond of purpose. If the paid staff or a handful of members can do it, it is an inadequate mission. Some argue that, if all the members can accomplish it together, it still may be inadequate. Perhaps the mission of a church should require the intervention of God. At any rate, it needs to challenge us to have faith and to feel renewed for being a part of it.

Over a long holiday weekend, one mainline congregation renovated twenty-three homes from which poor elderly residents were about to be evicted. When the task was done, a relatively new member said to her team leader, "God must have a very high opinion of us to have called us to do something so wonderful." In recent years the federal holiday celebrating the birth of Dr. Martin Luther King Jr. has been used as an occasion for churches and other organizations to come together for service projects. What an amazingly appropriate way of remembering the impact of that great soul's life. So too it is how we should commemorate the life and teachings of Jesus.

In many traditions, as pastoral candidates proceed through the steps of being credentialed, they are asked, often repeatedly, to describe their "call to ministry." This is, of course, an artificial construct because, for many, it is like asking people to describe the moment they reached adulthood or how they fell in love. What is most unfortunate is the implication that a clergy person has a "call" that nonprofessional ministers do not have. Everyone is called by the Spirit to learn, and grow, and love, and give. Our life is lived in answer to that call. The church's job is to nourish people as they answer their call. We do that through effective worship, the practices of the faith, and Christian community. The church's other job is to facilitate people who answer a call that has a value that cannot be measured in terms of financial worth.

A Proper-Sized Mission Will Challenge the Entire Congregation and, Perhaps, Require Them to Find Partners outside the Church

Many thriving churches find the vitality of their mission in partnerships. They partner with secular and community organizations to accomplish the kind of good Jesus did: healing the sick, relieving the oppressed, bringing good news to the poor and freedom to those in prison (Luke 4:18). As we partner with those who have expertise we lack, the hope is that our faith and peace and joy enliven their efforts. We don't have to tell them about Jesus so much as we need to be Jesus alongside of them. As we do that, we may find many unchurched disciples of Jesus who might like a church that actually shares their values and walks the talk.

The church too often seeks partners who believe what we believe. We might be much more effective if we sought out partners who care about what we care about. The Cathedral of Hope UCC in Dallas is known as the largest predominantly lesbian and gay congregation in the world. They determined many years ago that it was important that some of their mission work take them outside the United States so that they could have a greater impact and be actively reminded that God's children don't all live within these fifty states. It was also important that they do more than take a collection and send money. Their conviction was that, by going to help others, they would receive as many blessings as they gave and it would be a covenantal mission of mutuality, not an affluent North American church writing a check. Each of these mission projects was designed to do as much good as possible as defined by the people being served *and* to maximize the impact on those who went on the mission as well as those who stayed behind. Photographs and videos were essential to the project so those who could not go but could give also might be transformed.

One of their missions was to build schools and community buildings in the impoverished border town of Reynosa, Mexico.

After working there a few times, a Houston congregation contacted them about partnering. The Cathedral of Hope agreed because Reynosa needed all the help it could get. It was only after they all arrived for their first mission trip together that the Houston church discovered that their partners were mostly lesbian and gay. This very conservative, evangelical church did not believe the same things as the Cathedral did about homosexuality, but they did care about the same thing: the people of Reynosa. Ultimately, this mission project opened an amazing dialogue that resulted in the second church asking for information and rethinking what they believed about being lesbian or gay and Christian.

After years of debating with fundamentalists about homosexuality and the Bible, the leadership of the Cathedral of Hope adopted an aphorism from Mother Teresa of Calcutta: "Too many words. Just let them see what we do."

In his book *Well Connected*, Phil Butler defines partnership as "any group of individuals or organizations, sharing a common interest, who regularly communicate, plan, and work together to achieve a common vision beyond the capacity of the individual partners." Churches that are new or struggling have limited capacity, but through strategic partnerships the mission of highly effective organizations can become our mission, too. A very small congregation of migrant farm workers adopted "Ending hunger in the world" as its mission. With it, they honor the labor of most of the families in the congregation, plus they have partnered with Bread for the World, a faith-based national organization that not only feeds the hungry, but also works to change government policies that too often lead to hunger.

Effective partnerships can greatly expand the capacity of the congregation and can help transform both partners. Businesses are more likely to partner with progressive and inclusive churches because "saving souls" is not our agenda. That does not mean that who we are and what we care about is not an effective witness for Christ. Letting them see what we do and what we care about may be the only hope for rehabilitating the reputation that the public church has gotten in recent years. That is why it is critical to remember and remind people consistently that they are *not* volunteers; they are ministers. As ministers, they represent the church and they represent the God in whose name they are doing the ministry. Lots of organizations do good things. The church does what it does because we are the Body of Christ answering a call from God. As we give people an opportunity to live out their calling, they are changed and they become change agents for the Spirit.

The Mission Ought to Be a Twenty-First-Century Mission

Every time I visit an exciting and thriving church I come home with a dozen things that our church ought to be doing better or differently. Learning from others is critically important. To say that more strongly, when we fail to learn from others, we are guilty of the kind of hubris that is blasphemy of the Spirit because we are living as if the Spirit can move only in ways we understand and prescribe.

As we learn from one another, though, we always ought to be mindful of the fact that God is not calling us to be like someone else. Each church has a unique calling and needs to be both courageous and creative about answering it. I once visited a United Methodist Church near my hometown. It is perhaps the most progressive and inclusive mainline church in this small southern city. As I sat there on this particular Sunday, I noticed that a clown doll about two-feet-tall sat on the altar. That was peculiar enough, but the clown was green and, frankly, creepy. No reference was made to the clown and there was nothing in the bulletin explaining its presence.

A bit of online research uncovered that the clown indicates the fact that this church focuses on the arts, creativity, and celebration. It is the center of their logo and, with outstretched arms, looks a bit like a cross — an admittedly creepy cross. I think it is weird, and I am not one of the many people suffering from coulrophobia (fear of clowns). The church, however, located in an old, formerly dilapidated building in a marginal part of town, is amazing. The congregation was diverse, vibrant, and very energetic. The church, which almost had died, has been reborn and is one of the most vital churches I have visited. The newly renovated sanctuary was nearly full for an ordinary Sunday in Epiphany.

No, I don't get the clown, but apparently they do, which is what really matters. They have developed a unique and compelling mission that draws in the arts community, lesbian, gay, bisexual, and transgender folks, and equal numbers of young and old. They had the courage, in one of the oldest cities in America and in an traditional old building, to live into a mission that is unique and compelling. It has drawn a great deal of new life to a once moribund mainline church. My visits to other once-strong Methodist churches in this same city revealed that this congregation with its clown is definitely the exception in growth and vitality.

The challenge is that our pattern has been to go to a conference on creative worship at a church like this one and then go home and plop a creepy green clown down on the altar. (They actually may have liturgically correct clowns since the paraments for that Sunday were green also.) I can't imagine another mainline church in America where a clown on the altar would be a sign of renewal. (Notice my restraint. I am resisting all comments about clowns in the pulpit.) This can't be replicated, but this church does have much to teach us, not the least of which is to hear our unique call and follow it with passion.

Years ago, when Lyle Schaller was asked about why the world's largest lesbian, gay, bisexual, and transgender church was in, of all places, Dallas, he rattled off one of his famous lists in response. "You can build a mega-church of people who worship a hammer if you have (1) a compelling vision, (2) effective leadership, (3) compelling worship, and (4) a way for the congregation to respond." He was being a bit hyperbolic, of course, but his point is that giving a congregation a clear and unique opportunity to live out their mission is critical.

Many churches are forming 501(c)3 nonprofits as a tool for doing this. If the church's passion is significant, a separate non-profit may be effective. There are few grants that are available to churches but thousands available to faith-based nonprofits doing nonreligious work. In addition, many of our members work for corporations that will match an employee's charitable donations, though not to churches. The danger, of course, is diverting giving; however, this is not an issue if you also allow the nonprofit to absorb some of the expenses that the church generally has funded. The staff member who coordinates community outreach for the church can be paid, at least partially, by the nonprofit if the outreach is charitable but not overtly religious.

Use all the tools available for pursuing your congregation's unique mission and ministry. Recruit young people who might think outside the church house box and will bring social media and new tools to the work. Ask secular organizations to help you. Make sure the mission resonates with the future identity of the church not — or at least not just — the past.

Embrace Your Mission in Such a Way That People Are Changed

The leader of one marginalized congregation worked for years to improve the self-esteem of that congregation. Repeatedly telling them that they were beloved daughters and sons of the Living God had no impact. Refuting the arguments used to exclude them hardly reduced the doubt and fear at all. Whenever something went wrong in their lives, they almost instantly reverted to their fundamentalist roots, a time when they were taught that they were unlovable sinners who deserved hell. No intellectual appeal seemed to have the slightest impact.

The change in that community came almost incidentally. After mobilizing almost the entire membership to become genuine ministers doing the work Jesus would do, the pastor discovered that a side effect was a radical transformation of how people felt about themselves. While the lesson might be obvious, it took a while to recognize that if people want to feel good about themselves, they should be good people. The church should be giving people lots of opportunities to be good people. When the church gives everyone a chance to be a minister of the Gospel and an incarnation of the Spirit, an authentic transformation takes place. This isn't the self-esteem positive-thinking, but the transformation of a soul that sits exhausted and hears the Spirit whisper, "Well done good and faithful servant."

One footnote about this is the principle that a mirror is a great tool for developing or renewing a congregation, *if* you know which side to use. As the congregation begins to live into its mission, it is important for leadership to hold up a mirror. We are redefining, in most places and for most people, what it means to be the church of Jesus Christ. Showing videos of service projects, honoring those who serve as heroes, letting people bear witness to the impact in a meeting or worship time, all have great power in reinforcing the transformation. It also invites others into the process. Take every opportunity to celebrate visibly the fulfillment of the mission of the church and to make heroes out of those who are leading and participating. What gets rewarded in a system gets done.

These seven secrets only begin to explore the power of a compelling mission in a community of faith. Helping a church discover their unique mission and live into it is a vital function of transformational leadership. Ultimately, a church that keeps score of the number of lives helped, healed, and transformed has a mission that will be empowered by the Spirit and the world will rise up and call them blessed.

TEN

Transformational Worship

Enthusiasm is not the enemy of the intellect.
— Said of the critic Irving Howe

If mainline denominational churches could change only one thing about who they are and how they function, it should be worship. Furthermore, if we could get only this one thing right, the decline of the mainline church would cease because effective, powerful, transformational worship can be the engine that drives all the other worthy values and ministries of the church.

Worship is the front door through which our future enters. There are churches for whom that may not be true, but for now and the immediate future new people experience your church first in worship. Even in the emergent church, it is in the gathered community where people first, and most frequently, connect. So if you can fix only one thing, you might focus on worship. Conversely, if you fail to fix this one thing, all the hard work in all the other areas will have a significantly diminished effect. This is true because worship is:

- where you serve the largest number of your members

- where most of the Christian education, spiritual formation, and even pastoral care takes place

- the one place in our culture where life is rightly ordered. (Worship is where we put God at the center of our universe rather than living in an utterly egocentric world.)

This last point deserves a book unto itself. In fact, it should be the sociological and theological motivation for the entire church

171

seeking to shepherd a reformation of worship. There is little disagreement in any field of thought that the egocentrism of contemporary American culture is deadly on almost every level. It has led to the ongoing destruction of the environment and the continued unwillingness to make the sacrifices needed to change directions; it has led to the neglect of the most vulnerable of us, our children and our elders; it is the sole reason that health care in this country is a commodity, not a civil right; our militarism and xenophobia is rooted there — the list could go on and on. The remarkably wise and insightful writers of the Genesis parable recognized that this is literally the original sin. Our Hebrew forebears did everything in their power to teach us that, "There is one God...and we are not the One."

If for an hour or so a week, we can bring people to an experience of authentic worship, we may begin to recover the proper reordering of life with the One true God at the center. The Bible is consistent in its testimony that no one comes into the presence of the Living God and remains unchanged. Our challenge is to craft an experience that is unlike the experiences that folks get in any other place in their lives. The church will never be the best source of education, or music, or entertainment, or even social activism. Those are not our principal callings. What we alone can offer is an experience of the Divine. If people can encounter the God from whom they came and to whom they will return, they will be transformed and we will have fulfilled our principal calling. All our other mission and ministries radiate from the worship that is the heartbeat of the church.

Jesus reminded us that the first commandment was "to love God with all our heart, soul, mind and strength"; then, from *that*place, we will be able "to love our neighbors as we love ourselves." Culturally we seem determined to build our lives backward. We begin with loving ourselves, and, if there is anything left, we might love our neighbors. Loving God is at best a distant third. This is not a critique of the American education system or the American family; rather, the church bears the responsibility. Is your church a place where someone could walk in off the street and fall in love with God? If a person decided that something was missing in their life, and they gave your church a try one random Sunday morning, would they leave that time having touched the face of God, or felt the breath of the Spirit blow across their lives? If not there, where will they have such an encounter?

In part, our failure to offer transformational worship stems from neglecting the first commandment of Jesus. A visit to most modern mainline Protestant churches would leave you thinking that Jesus told us to love God with our mind and leave the rest of our being at home. There are altogether too few opportunities to love God with your heart or soul or strength in the average Protestant worship service. Our mental exercises have left people knowing more about things they could care less about, but when was the last time people caught their breath in one of your worship services? Perhaps worship, like life, should be measured by the breaths we miss, not the ones we take.

Progressive churches have turned worship into a largely cerebral experience. We can be classist and disdainful of our more evangelical sisters and brothers whose worship is altogether too emotional for our taste. As Marva Dawn points out in her book *Reaching Out without Dumbing Down: A Theology of Worship for these Urgent Times,* we can transform our worship without "dumbing it down." Her encouragement to reclaim some of our more ancient traditions is a piece of the strategy. However, we also must address our own inhibitions and class judgments that allow us to scream our heads off at sports events but keep us terrified to cheer the presence of God even internally in the sanctuary. Tears, laughter, and joy that burst spontaneously into applause all must be recalled from exile.

Ultimately we believe that people's lives would be transformed by an *experience* with God. What is certain is that our churches would be transformed because people are hungry for something transcendent, and, if we offered them that, they would line up like starving souls outside a soup kitchen. The need is so great and the hunger so profound that I believe if we can offer fifty-two transformational divine encounters a year people will beat a path to our door.

Of course there are a number of challenges to doing that:

1. Our worship is too often crafted for past, not future, congregations. We do what those who are now sitting in our pews expect, not what those who are seeking God need.

2. Worship is prone to miss the point. People don't really need to know more about God, they need to know God, to have an encounter with God. What does it say about a service where announcements take more time than prayer or praise?

3. We are creating worship for a post-Christian culture that doesn't know the language or references or reasons for what we do.

It isn't that they dislike what we believe or have to offer; we just have no common vocabulary, metaphors, or memories. We must stop assuming people know even the most basic facts or context for what we do in worship. Every element of every service must be evaluated through the eyes of someone who doesn't speak our language. Failing to do that is as excluding as any prejudice. Insider language is abusive inhospitality to those who naively are seeking God.

While the above list could go on, let's also add:

4. We now are crafting sermons and worship for a congregation with Attention Deficit Disorder.

We now create sacred experiences for people who communicate constantly by text message, make their daily confessions on Facebook, and quest for truth by surfing from one web page to another. For a younger congregation — regardless of the style — worship must be more fast-paced and without gaps or unintentional silences. Think radio, and you will rid your service of those times when the congregation sits silently, watching people walk to the lectern or pulpit or microphone. We are seeking to communicate the Gospel to people who know that when there is dead air something has gone wrong. When a service is not as moving and fast-paced as TV or radio or YouTube, this generation assumes that it is not as valuable or important.

Dr. Tom Long, addressing a group of multi-staff church senior pastors, was bemoaning the fate of narrative preaching, which assumes that a person falls in step with you at the first and, if you do it well, will walk with you until the end. Today, however, we are working with a culture that sees a park bench as we walk along and they sit down to explore something else, just like they would when a hyperlink on a website catches their attention.

Despite all of this, people still need the Lord. In a "Tweeting" world, communion with God is what is most needed. We must create worship and craft our sermons, lessons, and conversations with lots of re-entry points, assuming people have gotten distracted many times along the way. We also must avoid making negative judgments about those distractions and assume that the Spirit may be at work there too.

What does transformative twenty-first-century worship look like?

One of the clichés by which I live is "One size fits some." That is never truer than when it comes to worship. There are many roads to our destination. While we may cite examples of effective worship from one setting or another, it would be a mistake to hear that as advocating that all churches adopt that style. Effective worship is utterly dependent on our cultural context. What is effective in a historically African-American church may not work in a new Korean congregation where half the service is in English and half is in Korean. We all must follow the path that is appropriate in the part of the garden where we have been planted, but some underlying principles apply to us all.

Perhaps we should ask, What do all these various styles of effective worship have in common? What makes worship vital, vibrant, and transformational? What is the secret? There are many secrets, but we would like to lift up seven.

Know for Whom Worship Is Being Designed

This is very different from understanding the historic and cultural values of a congregation or the community they serve. Genuinely knowing your community is vital, but the truth is your church isn't going to appeal to the entire community and you couldn't accommodate them if it did. So whom are you called to serve? Too often inclusive churches try to be all things to all people and end up serving no one's needs well.

Mass marketing is increasingly ineffectual, especially if your resources are limited, but businesses have discovered that niche marketing can produce the results they desire. What is the niche in your community to which your church can effectively appeal? Whose needs can you meet? Who would be attracted to who, where, and what you are? If the people you would appeal to the most no longer live in that neighborhood, perhaps that is the issue that you must address first.

As you consider this, you must distinguish between the market you are reaching now and the market you need to reach. One thing that distinguishes churches that are doing transformational worship well is that they began to grow when they designed worship for the people who were *not* there, rather than the people who were. The late business guru and "social ecologist" Peter Drucker insisted that we ought to ask ourselves two questions:

1. What business are you in?

2. Who are your customers?

A critical lesson that must be integrated fully if our churches are to reverse their decline is that our customers are *not* our members; our customers are those who need God. One of the great challenges pastors and church leaders face is teaching congregations that *they* are the Body of Christ, and hence they are called by God to serve, *not* to be served. We are producers, not consumers; we are the hosts, not guests. Our job as leaders is to challenge people to take off their bibs and put on their aprons.

Congregations will resist change until they understand who it is God has called them to serve. As long as they believe they are guests rather than hosts, consumers rather than producers, they will believe worship should be designed for them. If a pastor tries to change worship without first teaching the congregation that they are the ministers to the community, the only thing the pastor is likely to transform is her or his work address.

It may be the ultimate irony (or it may be how God wove creation to be), but in congregations where the members understand that worship is not crafted for them but for those they are called to serve, the congregation seems to have the fullest and richest experience of worship themselves. Their shift in attitude is perhaps the strongest sign that they have begun to live out of a God-centric place. When that happens, worship becomes more than a Sunday-morning experience. It becomes an attitude toward life and eventually a lifestyle: God-neighbor-self.

Dying churches worship in a way that appeals to those who *used to* fill the pews; thriving churches worship in a way that appeals to those who *will* fill the pews. Countless mainline churches languish because their worship is designed for a congregation that fled to the suburbs long ago or died of old age. Often they complain that "no one lives around here anymore," when what is true is that the neighborhood is teeming with people the church could be serving. Unless boatloads of European immigrants flee once more to our shores, our congregations need to shape worship to meet the needs of the people who live here now, or we will die. Perhaps we deserve to die.

Historically, the bread of communion was called "the host." Worship must live into the reality that God is the host and our job is to ensure that everyone feels genuinely welcomed around the table.

Transformational Worship Is Congruent

Many of us have visited churches where the pastor obviously had attended a workshop in which he or she was taught to do worship a certain way. The congregation may be tolerant or even gamely trying to join in, but it just doesn't feel appropriate for that setting or those people. While young people are not attracted to boring worship, they will flee from anything that feels inauthentic.

Watching an all-white choir try to sway and clap on the downbeat while singing a song out of the African-American tradition can embarrass everyone and may not make African-Americans in the congregation feel included. There are many ways to deliberately weave threads of diverse traditions together and honor other styles, values, and voices, but it must be done with integrity. That is, it must be integrated authentically into the culture of the worshiping community. Education, conversation, and creating a space where diversity is a genuine core value are critical steps that must precede artificially contrived worship expressions. Patronizing is worse than exclusion. At least the excluding church is apparent in its prejudice. Artificially importing an expression or tradition from another culture without creating a value and a context disrespects that culture in an attempt to make the majority feel better about themselves. Diversity and inclusion should be authentic values for progressive churches. That is the hard work that must be done before we simply co-opt the traditions of others. Nothing is more beautiful than worship in which all voices are heard.

Worship also needs to be congruent with the space in which it takes place. A church that worshiped in a highly liturgical fashion was forced to meet for two years in an office complex while their new sanctuary was constructed. The office space where they met had low ceilings and folding chairs. In that space, a formal procession with a crucifer and torches seemed like a parody of the worship they valued. Despite their best efforts, the space lacked any beauty or gravitas, and while the regular worshipers who had experienced the liturgy in another setting could adapt, to first-time visitors, the high liturgy in that setting made it appear the congregation was "playing church." Fortunately, the leadership of that congregation highly valued the experience of the folks who visited, so they adapted their style of worship. The result: during their two years in the wilderness, the church grew by 27 percent in a space that was not at all conducive to their worship style.

Conversely, having a worship band in an old historic building may seem just as inauthentic (though some have done it successfully). For this reason, informal services may need to be held in fellowship halls, chapels, or other less formal spaces. Again, the style is not the point. Rather, the point is that the style is congruent with the congregation and where the congregation worships.

Being congruent must not be an excuse for being rigid or failing to evolve or change. In a city in the Deep South, college-age young people stream out of a three-hundred-year-old Episcopal church at 9:00 on Sunday night after attending Evensong, and a congregation of mostly undocumented immigrants attend a Spanish-language service every week at a historically lesbian and gay church in Texas. In a liturgical suburban church, vested clergy lead a "U2charist" with rock music blaring and lyrics projected on the walls. Worship integrity is about expressing integrated values, not about being locked forever into a certain style of worship.

Worship Deserves Our Best
Because God Deserves Our Best

There once was a day when people wore their best clothes to church on Sunday. In some settings that meant their best boots or hats or overalls, but worshipers tried to present themselves to God dressed in their best. As our culture has evolved, these values shifted. Today if a male pastor wore a suit, an uninformed observer might think he was a banker or lawyer, because those are about the only two careers in which men wear suits today. When many of us were growing up, our parents taught us to say, "Yes ma'am" and "No sir" to our elders. Those external expressions of respect and formality have all but disappeared. It can be debated whether this is good or bad, but it is clearly the situation in which we live. Worship is shaped against this background.

In some settings the formality of a liturgy that uses language, robes, music, and instruments that never would be found outside of church has become an effective tool for creating a transcendent experience. In that hour of worship, you hear sounds, say words, sing songs, see things, and perhaps even smell scents that you will encounter nowhere else. Hence you are invited into a unique experience with the One and only God. In other places, the value that is most important is the immanence of God: in every moment of our lives God is present. To make that clear, the language and dress and experience of worship is such that it becomes impossible to tell when the technical service begins and ends. The congregation is invited out of their routine where God is present into a few moments of spiritual renewal where God is present; they are sent forth, back into their lives, as expressions of the fact that God is present.

Both of these, and a variety of others, are valuable and legitimate ways to approach worship. The key is that, for either to be effective, they must share one common trait: they must be done very well. Speech teachers often say that extemporaneous speeches require the most preparation to be effective. So too spontaneity is hard work if it is to be meaningful. Formal services that fall into repetitious routine are as ineffectual as casual services that have not been adequately prepared for those who will be present.

The greatest struggle probably occurs in the traditional middle-of-the-road, white, European style of the majority of Protestant churches. This is largely because the worship is shaped out of routine or tradition. Assumptions are made that everyone present understands and appreciates what is being done and why, so little thought or effort is given to enlivening the liturgy or helping to make it more stimulating and relevant. Although pastors were taught in seminary that the word "liturgy" means "work of the people," few people put adequate work into making the liturgy germane and meaningful. It isn't easy, and it won't happen accidentally.

Young people grew up watching movies and television and listening to music where no expense was spared to achieve precisely the desired effect. Timing is impeccable and to the millisecond. When worship is sloppy, ill prepared, or ineffectual, the assumption must be that it isn't important or valuable. Even casual worship must stir the heart and call us to be "lost in wonder, love, and grace." Miscues are inevitable, but when they are more frequent in church than at a concert, which one is more important is clear to the un-churched. When amateur theater has better production values than divine worship, we have sent a clear message about which one is more important. Casual worship can be very effective, but sloppy and ill-prepared worship never is, regardless of the style.

Worshiping God is the most important thing we do every week; leading people into the presence of God is our highest privilege. It deserves our best effort and our hardest work. Whether you are buying a sweater or a car, it is the quality of the work that gives it value. Whether you are eating a hamburger or dim sum, it is the chef's attention to detail and the effort extended that make it obvious that your experience is important. Commercial establishments spare no expense or effort to shape the kind of experience you will have when you visit them. We who are charged with being hosts to those who will gather for worship need to ensure that they know we did all in our power to prepare a place for them and that we have worked hard so that they will have the best possible experience.

It is true that no matter what we do we alone cannot create an experience of genuine worship; however, by our neglect, sloppiness, or lassitude, we certainly can hinder the gathered community from having the opportunity to be transformed by worship. If we honor our responsibility and give worship preparation our best effort, God can be relied upon to do the rest.

Seek to Touch Both the Head and the Heart

Regardless of the style, effective worship experiences all have elements of drama, mystery, energy, and movement. They are designed to weave together an experience for contemporary people. Too often worship is designed by and for people who grew up watching the old TV show *Bonanza*. The entire show was done with essentially four sets, and we sat and stared at them for an hour. The people we need to communicate with today grew up watching computer animation that uses forty sets a minute. Effective worship must have energy and movement, passion and power. It must be clear that those who lead worship care deeply about the One worshiped and the congregation that has gathered.

Liberal preaching and worship frequently have been intellectual exercises. We sing historic hymns, read ancient texts, and practice treasured liturgy, but rarely does a tear fall or a heart flutter. Emotionalism has been disdained and those faith traditions that practiced it have been regarded as inferior on almost every level. Today we understand that attitude to be both classist and perhaps even racist, yet that style of worship persists in most mainline churches. They would be horrified to be considered either classist or racist, but they still exclude those who desire to worship with their hearts. Perhaps what is most needed is for the passion of the evangelical and Pentecostal traditions to be coupled with the intellectual rigor of the progressive mainline church.

Shouldn't worship move you at least as often as it informs you? Blockbuster movies, bestselling novels, award-winning television shows all touch the human heart. Why on earth shouldn't worship? If people's lives were transformed by information alone then every Ph.D would be a saint. With the advent of the Internet, almost every piece of information ever known is available to us, but we are not significantly happier or healthier or more spiritual people.

Worship Should Be as Sensual as We Can Make It

Although Jerusalem and Athens are only seven hundred miles away from each other, the philosophies that they gave to the world are light years apart. The Greeks taught that the physical world was inferior to the spiritual realm. They believed that the soul was eternal and that the physical body was just a temporary shell to be left behind. In fact, they saw the physical nature of life as a hindrance to becoming more spiritual. When Socrates came to the time of his dying, he rejoiced that his soul at last would be free of what he called "the prison house of his body."

To the Greeks, the soul and body were separate and unequal. This apparently is still the philosophy that dominates the way many fundamentalist Christians look at life. However, it is not what the Hebrew faith taught, and it is clearly not what Jesus lived out or believed. The foundation of our Judeo-Christian faith is the creation story with which the Bible begins, when God created all that is and pronounced it good, very good. Quickly reading through the Gospels, one is struck immediately by the reality that Jesus was just as concerned with healing bodies that were broken as redeeming souls that were lost.

The Greek heresy that divides life into the physical and the spiritual has infiltrated our thought in many negative and devastating ways — like our being a sex-negative society. One Roman Catholic excuse for not ordaining women is that a woman might have to serve at the altar during the time that she is menstruating. The implication is that there is something shameful or impure about a woman's normal bodily functions. In the first biblical parable about sin, Adam and Eve became ashamed of their bodies only after they sinned. Our experience of shame is always rooted in our brokenness. How much of our neglect and abuse of the environment is connected to the endemic sexism that infects so much of Christianity, Judaism, and Islam? We speak of "Mother Earth," and men of power or wealth or influence proceed to use and abuse creation in the same way that we too often have used and abused women. Sexism is rooted in the belief that men are created in the image and likeness of God, but somehow women are a secondary creation. To most people of faith, God is our Father, and the earth is referred to as mother, clearly one with power over the other. The doctrine of the incarnation and the resurrection, however, both clearly remind us of the sacred and eternal nature of all creation.

How can Christians not be radical environmentalists? After all, the Bible teaches that "the earth is the Lord's and the fullness thereof, the world and all that dwell therein." We who are Christians or Jews believe that we all have been called to be a part of the oldest profession. That's right: gardening. According to that first parable, God created humans of the stuff of the earth, breathed into us the breath of life, placed us in a garden, and said, "Take care of it for me." For thousands of years, we have tended the garden, and the earth has provided for our every need. Now, though, we are like a greedy farmer eating his seed corn, or a selfish gardener poisoning her own land. How we treat the earth is bearing a harvest of great grief for us. As Albert Schweitzer said, "Until humans can extend the circle of their compassion to include all living things, they will never, themselves, know peace."

The incarnation is a core Christian truth, so how do we make our worship more incarnational, more sensual? Again, remember that "one size fits some." While this is an over-simplification, it is important to remember that our congregations are made up of people who are:

+ Auditory
+ Visual, or
+ Emotive

Of course, all people communicate in all three ways, but most of us experience life more in one way or another. So if we are going to communicate the Gospel effectively, we must try to use all three approaches in our worship. Sensual worship is very important, and, when possible, it should appeal to all our senses. We all have had the experience of having a smell transport us somewhere. That may be as simple as using peach-scented room deodorizer when you talk about how peach trees require thirty hours of freezing weather to bear fruit; or rose-scented spray when you talk about the Rose of Sharon or are playing Bette Midler's song "The Rose" to make a point. During that season when we read the passage in which Jesus called himself the "Bread of Life," you could put a breadmaker in the sanctuary the night before. Watering mouths and growling stomachs transport us back to Jesus' first listeners who were just a meal or two away from starvation.

Experiential worship is designed for the whole person. It is something we all can do, but admittedly we all probably need help. We need to recruit a team of people to help us think this way and help us find the resources to make worship a powerful, transformational experience. No one will be more moved than the team who helped you make it happen. Imagine the theater director who was told he was going to hell by the conservative church of his childhood now able to bring his art to helping you shape worship. Recruit the woman who loved doing magic tricks, but was told it was Satanic, to help you create spontaneous fire on Pentecost.

As we anticipate Sunday we should ask:

+ What do we want people to feel in this service?

+ What images should they take away?

+ What should they smell?

+ What do we want them to hear?

+ What do we want them to leave this service and do?

This brings us to the sixth secret of transformational worship.

True Worship Requires a Response

The oldest rhythm of the church is that we gather to be nourished and renewed, and then we are scattered to serve. Every service should remind people that they are the true ministers of the church, that they are God's people and are called by God, valued by God, and empowered by God. Worship should end with a reminder that the time for their service has begun.

A church leader's job is to craft fifty-two experiences each year in which people encounter God, feel God's love for them, are cleansed by forgiving grace, and challenged to become all they were created to be, and then to set them loose on an unsuspecting world. As people of faith live in response to transformational worship they change the world, and they also are changed for good and forever.

Neglecting this rhythm has been deadly for the church. We have focused on membership and meeting the needs of our members. The result is that we have become a dying club. Again, a cursory study of scripture reveals that as people encounter the living God they are changed and, almost every time, they are sent to do something to change the world.

Beginning in the 1970s, many mainline services were rearranged so that the service no longer ended with the sermon, a hymn and the benediction. A more ancient form of worship was reclaimed in which the congregation was offered an opportunity to respond to the Word of God read and proclaimed. More and more mainline churches are offering communion weekly. Others are finding ways to surround the reading of scripture with significance. A lay person who worshiped regularly with a congregation that sang a gradual before the Gospel was read, then stood for the reading and sang a glory in response, attended another church from a reformed tradition. She observed that while that denomination claimed to be "people of the Word," they did nothing to indicate that what they read was important at all. Her observation was, "When they read the Gospel, it was like they had laid an egg out on a limb. They didn't bother even trying to build a nest." We who are "people of the Word" need opportunities to respond to God's great good news to us, both within worship and when it ends.

Multiple Services with Diverse Styles Work Well

Many, if not most, Protestant churches worship in a style that was shaped by the culture of a general store where almost everyone in the community shopped and out of which most of the community's needs were met. That general store approach simply doesn't work for people who grew up shopping at malls with hundreds of specialty stores. It is even less effective for a culture where almost every store in the world can be accessed on the Internet. Think of the variety of restaurants available. Even small towns now have establishments that offer cuisines from around the world. Why on earth do we in the church continue to think that everyone's needs can be met by a single style of worship?

To return to an earlier analogy, mainline churches are like beautiful flower gardens. We have great buildings, a powerful heritage, and wonderful, devoted, and faithful people. The world certainly needs more flowers, music, beauty, and art. The trouble, though, is that people are spiritually hungry, and they can't live on flowers. They are hungry for vegetables, and we need to be planting vegetable gardens. The beauty and tradition of our worship certainly meets the needs of many, but we also need to find a way to meet the needs of those who hunger for something different.

The mistake we too often make is that, out of fear or sometimes desperation, we decide to rip out the flowers and plant vegetables. Perhaps what might be more effective is tending the flowers while using much of our time, resources, and energy to plant vegetables. Our world needs both. The trouble is we are pretty good with flowers, but we don't know much about growing the vegetables that twenty-first-century people need.

We must recruit and train pastors and leaders to be hospice chaplains *and* new church obstetricians simultaneously, to tend the flowers, but creatively plant some vegetables. This is difficult, but not nearly as difficult as training our pastors to resurrect the dead. The first step to a solution for any problem is to think differently about the problem, and that is what I've been inviting us to do.

It is true that worship that meets the needs of younger families with children often doesn't meet the needs of older people who also need the Lord. The noise and chaos does indeed make it impossible for our older members to hear. Unfamiliar music with strange rhythms and casual language is not moving to them. People from different generations have different needs, and no one deserves to be made to feel bad about that.

The solution is that we *all* may have to plant a new church. You may have to plant a new church within your existing church. That may be as simple as starting an alternative worship service, but if your church is to have a future beyond the funeral dates of your current members, you will have to do something different.

The very definition of crazy is doing the same thing and expecting different results. That is never truer than when it comes to worship. As Lyle Schaller likes to say, "If we wake up tomorrow and it is 1950 again, our church is ready." If, however, we wake up tomorrow and it is the twenty-first century, we have to begin living and working and worshiping in the twenty-first century.

People still need an experience with the living God. Our job is to shape a worship service that gives it to them, not to continue expecting them to change in order to find what we are doing meaningful. It is time for our worship services to take off our bibs and put on our aprons.

ELEVEN

Leading Congregations to Change

If you keep doing what you've always done,
you will keep getting the results you've always gotten.
Can you live with that?

Seventeenth-century scientist Sir Isaac Newton, in his first law of motion, observed that "an object at rest tends to remain at rest." He might have drawn this conclusion while watching a pastor trying to persuade a congregation to make some needed changes. Inertia, resistance, denial, and apathy all can be much more aggressively powerful forces than their passivity implies. As Jimmy Dugan, portrayed by Tom Hanks in *A League of Their Own*, says, "If it was easy, everyone would be doing it." If change was easy, our churches already would have made the changes necessary to grow and thrive and be transformational forces. If it was easy, leadership wouldn't be necessary, and your job would be eliminated.

Change isn't easy, and while it does occur naturally in many settings, churches tend to consciously or unconsciously put into place systems and structures to resist change. Ironically, their resistance to change can be so great that they are willing to change leaders rather than embrace the life-giving changes that are needed. Leaders underestimate the level of change resistance at their own peril. This is why we all need to be trained to be change-agents if we are to be effective and long-term leaders.

It is tempting to believe that all we really need to do is explain the circumstances and people then will do what is best. If you believe this, then your doctor has never tried to get you to lose weight, stop smoking, exercise more, or worry less. Those changes all are good for your body. We know the facts. We've all seen people die because they failed to make these changes. We love our children and grandchildren and want to live long and healthy lives. So how easy has it been to change your diet, your work habits, or your sedentary lifestyle? We all have made changes and then fallen right back into bad patterns. Permanent changes are tough for individuals and churches. Perhaps remembering our own failures will make us more patient with our struggling congregation and will keep us from unrealistic optimism about just how difficult real and lasting change is. It can be done, but if it was easy then everyone would do it.

So what are the seven secrets to successful transformation?

No Solos Allowed

A new or renewed leader is almost always the catalyst that initiates change. However, it is critical that we understand the word "catalyst." Think of Jesus' example of yeast. A little yeast can leaven the whole loaf, but it does so from within and begins by transforming the dough immediately surrounding it.

The first stage in leading change effectively is recruiting leadership partners and helping them acquire the skills and insights necessary to take this perilous journey into the unknown with you. While you may have a clear vision of your destiny, the journey is very unpredictable. When you sail into rough waters, you need a trustworthy crew fully prepared to do their jobs and keep the ship safe and on course. Again, it is not a question of if you hit resistance, but when. If you are the only one trained to sail the vessel, then even small storms of resistance can throw you off course.

Recruit people who can be your natural allies and train them about what to expect. No one should be surprised by resistance, and no one should take it personally if they know its source. A team of well-trained leaders will find resistance to be a good sign that progress is being made and things are taking their natural course. Untrained partners tend to panic and add to the anxiety because they don't know want to expect. Your job is to recruit people who can be a nonanxious presence effectively. Coach them to avoid didactic conversations and seek to inject a spirit of hopefulness that calms anxiety rather than promotes polarization.

In other words, you don't need a team of people to argue the case for change; you need partners who can help create a spirit of trust, hope, and optimism in the community. It is more important that they understand the dynamics of change than that they understand the specifics of the change itself. As often as not, it isn't what you are proposing that is experiencing resistance but change that is producing anxiety. The most significant influencers in a community can better serve as a nonanxious presence than as subject-matter experts. During a storm, most people don't need an explanation about thermodynamics; they need a calm and trusted voice to assure them that it all will be okay. As you anticipate making vital changes, begin by identifying, recruiting, and training a small group of partners who will help you navigate the anxiety ahead. Done well this will be one step you may later think you didn't need to take because the storms never became apparent. Neglected, the journey may be lost before you ever have a chance to sail out of the harbor.

Grieve the Myth

The myth that keeps most churches on the road to decline is that "healthy churches are free of conflict." That is a lie. Dying churches are free of conflict. Of course, this does not mean that conflict can't be unhealthy and kill a church, but we are called to be leaders for the living, not chaplains holding the hands of a dying church. In other words, your goal is *not* to keep everyone happy. The sooner you grieve and get over that myth, the quicker you can get on with the changes that will save your church and empower it to save the hurting and hopeless in your community.

Change brings inevitable conflict and chaos, but if you believe conflict and chaos are not of God, go back and read the Bible, starting with Genesis, in which God creates out of chaos. Jesus did not send us into the world to "be nice." If conflict avoidance was the sign of a good person then Jesus was pure evil. If being conflict free is the sign of a healthy church then the church in Acts was a complete failure. Conflict emerged the instant the church was born. "These are drunk with wine" was the accusation leveled at the church that was only minutes old. Already, misunderstanding and accusation.

Peter's first sermon was delivered in defense of the changes the Spirit was making. While no one enjoys conflict or deliberately seeks it, do not judge it as the absence of the Spirit. When the wind of God blows, all manner of things get stirred up; do not mistake the chaos as being a failure of the Divine. It is, in fact, an opportunity for the Spirit to move across the face of the deep, creating something new and alive.

One of the things with which we all must make peace is that change will create conflict, and the conflict can be a gift of the Spirit. Our job as leaders is to remain nonanxious, remind the congregation that this is not the first time God's people have struggled with the dynamics of change, and reassure them that the God of rainbow, cloud, and fiery pillar still lives and will be with them on this journey. Some, perhaps many, will want to go back. As much as we want to keep everyone happy and everyone on board, some inevitably will leave. Our job as leaders is to remember that the changes we are making are so that others will join us and, thus, we will fulfill the call of God.

Long-term pastors can tell stories about how they lost a family or a group of members and feared the church would die, only to discover that their departure opened the door for others to join. It is not that the departing folks were wrong or bad, but that their leave was change and allowed for change that brought new growth. Every pastor squirms a bit when the lectionary reading comes around to John 15, and we are forced to deal with the idea of pruning for new growth. We all are trained and oriented to plant, water, and fertilize, but pruning is not in our DNA. As Jesus said, however, it is in God's DNA, and who are we to resist the will of God?

As we prepare our churches for change, we must prepare them for inevitable conflict. We must see it, just as every healthy relationship must, as an inevitable part of authentic love and growth together. Our role as leaders is to facilitate the conflict as life-giving and not allow it to become destructive and life-threatening. We must be the ones to:

+ Speak the truth

+ Facilitate honest, healthy dialogue so that all are heard

+ Keep a sense of humor alive

+ Constantly remember the ultimate goal

+ Keep hope alive

+ Remind all that God's call trumps our comfort (see Exodus)

+ Celebrate the victories and common joys.

There are consultants, trainers, and limitless resources that can help us learn to deal with the anxiety, resistance, and conflict that are inevitable with authentic change. Simply acknowledging that these are normal and healthy parts of sacred relationships is half the battle. How many marriages died premature deaths because couples were conflict-avoidant too long or because they thought healthy couples didn't fight? One of the greatest witnesses of the Bible is its honesty. Holy people disagree, conflicts are constant, and God works miracles through it all. M. Scott Peck, in a lecture about relationships, said that there really are only two reasons for marriage: children and the friction. He contends that we cannot be healthy and whole people without the friction that comes from conflict and the change that it creates. Congregations are in covenant relationships with one another and with God. Friction is a healthy sign that the covenant is authentic, not superficial or artificially sweetened.

Conflict is not only a natural result of change; it is a catalyst for authentic change. Like the leaven, you don't need too much. Some is essential, however; otherwise, the dough will remain unchanged. Leaders must acquire the skills to help congregations navigate the stormy water, but first and foremost leaders must find the courage to sail into those waters. We must grieve the myth that "good churches don't fight." The truth is every relationship has conflicts. Healthy relationships are strong because of the changes that result from the conflict. Leaders cannot avoid conflicts, but they do cast the deciding vote for what the consequences are.

Pastors play an important role in helping congregations grieve the myths that are rooted in the past and in the fantasy that things aren't as bad as they seem. Again, as Lyle Schaller says, if we wake up and tomorrow and it's 1950, our churches are totally prepared to do vital and vibrant ministry. Our buildings are properly configured, our programming and priorities are perfectly aligned, and baby boomers are going to stream to our churches to raise their children with a proper Protestant education. However, if we wake up tomorrow in the second decade of the twenty-first century, then almost everything is going to need to change. There is a lot of grieving associated with the loss of the past in the one place that managed to hang on to it for half a century.

Pastors can comfort and encourage people in their grief; however, it is critical that lay leadership speak the truth. Sooner or later, even the kindest and most compassionate doctor must tell the truth about the patient's condition and prognosis. My mother always said that to know the truth but not tell it was the same as lying. Then she would add, "Christians don't lie." Well, my mother never tried to lead a church to renewal. Denial is treated as a sacrament, but it will not serve anyone well.

Tell the truth, challenge the myth, move ahead with hope. As with any other loss, there will be stages of grief, and one of those stages will be anger. Leadership means knowing that the anger isn't personal and accepting it as the price of truly leading.

Speak the truth and do so in as many different ways as possible. Remember: there are decades of denial to break through. Only when a congregation has worked through to acceptance is real change possible. Leaders are the first people who must grieve the congregation's mythology and accept the truth. Then it is their role to help the congregation do the same.

Create a Sense of Urgency

John Kotter, in his book *Leading Change* says that establishing a sense of urgency is a crucial first step to gaining needed cooperation. He suggests that in a company with a hundred employees at least a dozen must be motivated to go far beyond their routine efforts if change is to take effect. That number may be slightly higher in voluntary organizations. It may be that 25 percent of the membership must get a sense of urgency in a church before change will begin to happen.

In a paper titled "Leading Change in a Local Church," Gregg Waddell refers to the necessity of "unfreezing" the system. He writes:

> The most common mistake in change agency is to skip this step and introduce innovation before people recognize that they need it. This is like planting seed before plowing the earth or painting a car before applying the primer coat. There are things that have to happen or else the innovation will inevitably fail to take root. Leaders will almost certainly be faced with immediate and powerful resistance — similar to the physical body's natural immune system kicking in — if change is introduced without such preparation. Contrary to what some may think, change management does not consist merely of introducing change. Before the introduction of innovation, the old must first be unfrozen. The process of change begins with unfreezing the current situation and releasing the church from the forces that

bind her, so she can respond effectively to her environment. So how does this unfreezing take place? What can the leader do to unfreeze the congregation from its current configuration?

Creating a sense of urgency may be done in most situations by a frank description of the current situation and the resulting trajectory. As when a physician does a physical on a dying patient, the numbers speak the truth, especially when contrasted with the numbers of a healthy and thriving patient. In other, stronger situations, the change that is needed may not be of a life-threatening nature, but of a life-enhancing nature. For example, mental dexterity exercises have been proven to retard mental decline in the elderly and even in those with Alzheimer's. It isn't that the person must change or die, but the quality of life and what that person can contribute back to life is greatly enhanced by certain changes. Time and timing are critical factors in both situations, though. You cannot delay; lifestyle changes must take place now. With each passing day, the change is more difficult and ultimate impact diminished.

To continue our sailing imagery, a sense of urgency is the place where the wind of the Transforming Spirit meets our sails. The tension that is created there becomes the power to move the ship along even when the seas become turbulent. The authors of the book *Leading Congregational Change*, say that, "Urgency is critical in the individual congregation. It creates a driving force that makes the organization willing to accept change and to challenge the conventional wisdom." The trouble, of course, is that most mainline denominations lack completely any sense of urgency. Perhaps this is where our interpretation of apocalyptic literature fails us. We have abandoned the message of urgency, along with the understanding of historicity.

As agents of change, we are charged with the dual, and sometimes conflicting, roles of providing our congregations with enough hope and comfort to withstand the destructive forces of their anxiety and enough tension to create a vibrant sense of urgency that something new must be born. Our role as creators of change is both to calm and comfort the mother in the midst of perhaps the most painful experience of her life and urge her to willfully push for new life to be born.

Creating a sense of urgency in many settings requires a significant dose of truth telling, and we may need to begin with ourselves and our leadership. How do we have to change if we are to live fully into the mission of God for our lives and our church? Leadership that is willing to consider new possibilities without rushing to judgment may discover that the change that is needed begins in them. Nothing is more fascinating in the story of the early church than watching the leaders change as they sought to follow the wind of the Spirit as it blew across their world. They had to learn new ways of thinking and new ways of being as the Spirit brought people into the church whom the early leaders never even knew existed.

Our sense of urgency must be driven by a newly energized passion for the lost and those who are dying without Christ. While that sentence may have been spoken by a Southern Baptist or some other evangelical, it is the passionate conviction of one who does not believe in a literal hell, but who has walked with souls who live in a daily hell. Perhaps mainline pastors lack a sense of urgency because they spend too much of their time holding the hands of "nice" people. If we don't believe that people need the grace and forgiveness and hope of the Gospel then we have not had coffee with a single mother whose father told her that God was punishing her for getting pregnant out of wedlock. Our pretty buildings are surrounded by tragedies and trauma and fear and desperate needs that we are called by Jesus to address. Hell is very real, and people right outside our doors can bear witness to its torment. Our churches lose their sense of urgency when they become so self-absorbed that the color of the new carpet in the parlor takes up more of our passion and time than how to help the homeless teenagers on our streets. Our job as spiritual leaders is to challenge people to care about the things that Jesus cared about so deeply that the threat of death itself would not deter him.

A crisis can create a sense of urgency, but often our churches are like the frog in the pot on which the temperature has been gradually raised. By the time we are aware of the threat to our lives it is too late. In comfortably middle-aged and middle-classed mostly white churches the sense of social urgency is also absent. Mission trips and experiential ministry can help change that. Facilitating personal interaction with people in genuine need and crisis can help foster a sense of urgency. The bottom line is that we have to move folks out of their comfort zones. If the threat is not personal or imminent there will be little urgency, unless, of course, we can help a congregation fully embrace its identity as the Body of Christ. The best sense of urgency arises from an overwhelming need to live as Jesus would in the community where God has placed them.

Have a Vision Powerful Enough to Transform

My definition of vision is nothing more than "articulating God's preferable future." Jesus taught us that we ought to pray for "God's reign to come, God's will to be done, on earth as it is in heaven." Clearly we do not live in a world where God's will is always done, so it is the subject of our prayers and our life's efforts. While it is presumptuous to claim to know the will of God in all matters, as disciples of Jesus, there are many ways in which God's will for humankind, and for us, is clear.

There have been a number of books written that suggest that the role of the modern pastor of a thriving church is that of principal visionary. God speaks to and through the senior pastor to the people of God. There is no doubt that in certain settings this centralized and hierarchal model is efficient and, by some standards, effective in mobilizing people to work toward a single goal. However, as Peter Senge observed in his book *The Fifth Discipline*, many companies (and churches) have found that "lofty visions alone fail to turn around a firm's fortunes."

Fred Craddock often said that "good preaching is not so much speaking to people as it is speaking for people." By that he meant that good preaching isn't when people are awed by the preacher's wisdom and insight, but when they are allowed to discover their own. In the church, a visionary leader is one who helps the people discover the vision for their church that they already treasure in their hearts, and then to organize and articulate that vision back to them.

Leaders help a church ask, "Who are we?" "What are we called to do?" "What Spirit inspired dream burns in our hearts?" "Who would we be if all God's dreams for us came true?" "Who would we be if we were instruments in God's dreams for our community coming true?" Churches can answer these questions for themselves — if given the opportunity. Hearing their vision in their own voice is powerful. It is also important because, if the vision is genuinely God-given, it will require a great number of changes and significant sacrifice. That is much more likely if it is *their* vision than if you try to deliver it from on high. Leadership is facilitating the people to articulate their vision and then helping them to clarify it and develop a strategy around making it a reality.

Perhaps, as Kirk Hadaway suggests, transformational vision is not so much showing people where they need to go, as it is helping them to see who they are and who they can be. In *Behold I Do a New Thing,* Hadaway cites All Saints Episcopal Church in Pasadena as an example of how a progressive, radically inclusive congregation was, and is, empowered by what he calls their "vow" rather than their "vision."

> What they call their job and what I call a vow is this: *On behalf of Jesus Christ to dismantle all structures of injustice.* Dismantling injustice is not a vision or corporate goal — it is an intention and a direction that leads to specific actions. It is a vow, even a "covenant" with the world. Rather than following a vision, we give ourselves vision — the ability to see — and then we act accordingly (and resolutely).

That is powerful, but, as a strategy for change, vision may need to mean more than just that, or maybe it just needs more fleshing out, at least for some of us. Neuro-Linguistic Programming is not without accurate criticism, but the way that it frames how different people are motivated can be insightful. For example, it describes how some people are "move-away-from" people and others are "move-toward." Without judgment, it is simply an observation that some people are most powerfully motivated by their fears while others are motivated by possibilities. It is simply the old carrot/stick insight. Some people work really hard because they don't want to be poor. Some people work really hard because they want to be rich. In both cases, the result is hard work, so one is not better than the other. Some people are spiritually motivated by hell/threat/danger; others are spiritually motivated by heaven/reward/promise.

Again, it is important to remember that "one size fits some." You need to know which you are and then remember that not everyone is motivated as you are. Some people will need you to clearly, consistently, and frequently paint a compelling picture of the preferable future into which God is calling your church. Others will need to hear regularly and persuasively an outline of the dangers posed by our failure to make the needed changes and answer the call of God. The vision will need to be visual, auditory, and emotive. Everyone will need to see it, hear it, and feel it, but it will be more powerful for some in one form or another.

John Kotter defines vision as "a picture of the future with some implicit or explicit commentary on why people should strive to create that future." He then goes on to suggest three purposes vision serves in a change process:

1. Vision the direction for change; it allows for the organization of the details of our journey together.

2. Vision motivates people to take action in the same direction.

3. Vision coordinates the actions of individuals in a remarkably fast and efficient way.

To that, I would add a fourth. If it is the congregation's vision and is fully owned, it will motivate the elimination of some of the organizational restraints. An externally compelling vision stands powerfully against the bureaucracy that Edward de Bono defines in his book *I Am Right and You Are Wrong* as "an organization put together for a purpose, but coming to survive for its own sake." To cut through those constraints, the vision must be too powerful and compelling to be allowed to die of strangulation. Again, you will meet much greater success if a congregation must choose between *their* vision and *their* organizational restraints.

You Can't Communicate Too Much

Change lives and dies by effective communication. It is imperative that the greatest number of people is involved in formulating the biggest picture. If the change is comprehensive, every member needs to be invited to participate right from the start. This can be done in various ways, and given the schedules of people today, it probably needs to be done in a wide variety of ways. Ultimately, holding small group meetings in various places and at various times is probably most effective. In large gatherings it is impossible to ensure full participation. With a series of small group gatherings, however, you can ensure that everyone has the opportunity to attend. By going around the room, every person is offered a chance to speak. They also may pass. Either way, the choice is theirs. Even if they pass, they are given a chance to email their thoughts. If the change redefines the future of the church, it is imperative that none feel that they were not invited to participate.

Of course, once all have had a chance to have their say, your job will be to begin to consolidate and organize their thoughts into a comprehensive picture of God's preferable future. You then will want to have your leadership team work through it with you so that they will feel some responsibility for how it was shaped. The final edit should be made by those who are most skilled and knowledgable.

As the vision is formulated, you might think about concentric circles that move from the outside in. Once the vision is formulated, the strategy is developed from the inside out. Again, communication happens in concentric circles. Staff or mission-critical leadership should be fully briefed on all the strategic details. The larger the number to whom you are communicating, the bigger the picture that needs to be communicated. Ultimately, you will need to be able to communicate the big picture for the future to those who know nothing about the church. It should be crafted to be so compelling that it would make those who do not know you want to find out more.

Until every active member is sick of the vision, you have not even begun to communicate with the larger community. In most churches the pastor is the chief communication officer, so it is her responsibility to work the message of transformation into every sermon, email, article, prayer, and announcement. He must be relentless and incredibly creative in how the message gets repeated. This will require enlisting the assistance of many different groups in the church. The team that works on Internet communication likely will be very different from the one that produces printed material.

We tend to think of communication as the next stage in the process of change; however, it is also the catalyst that creates the change. On some levels it is the change itself. This is particularly true if it is a genuine paradigm shift for the identity of the church. Michael Foss, senior pastor of Prince of Peace Lutheran Church in Burnsville, Minnesota, did a great job of documenting the process his congregation went through as they moved from membership to discipleship. While there are a variety of reasons this particular shift wouldn't be appropriate for most progressive congregations, what is helpful is seeing how it happened and the transformations that took place along the way. In *Power Surge,* Pastor Foss talks about visiting DreamWorks Studio in Hollywood and the Disney Institute in Orlando. In both places, the thing that struck him was that the vision of who they are, where they are going, and who they are to become along the way was communicated consistently and persistently. It is expressed over and over in every possible way, until it isn't memorized but integrated. The vision literally becomes a part of the fabric out of which the institution is made. Ultimately you *cannot* over-communicate. Foss writes:

> Simply communicating the vision once, twice, or even thrice is not enough. We must plant the vision deep in the heart of the mission of the church and deep in the hearts of those who come to church. That is to say, we must weave it into the very fabric of our self-understanding as Christians. Purpose breeds personal power. The purpose of the Christian church — "faith active in love" — when connected to the lives of individual and family disciples is incredibly empowering.

When the people on the street know who your church really is and where it is going, you will know that you have done an adequate job of communicating to your congregation. They literally must internalize it so that it is a part of who they are. Moving a congregation toward a vision that has been so fully embraced is much easier because they are willing to change whatever it is that may be an impediment.

Root Change in Spiritual Practices

Please note that this is not a list of the seven steps of leading change. This is not the sixth thing that you do, nor is it the sixth most important thing that must be done. In fact, some would suggest that this is the first and most important step. Churches that have used Martha Grace Reese's material have found her suggestion that they should begin with a season of prayer to be her most powerful point.

Imagine for a moment the transformative power of asking the congregation to have no meetings of any kind for ninety days but to spend that time fasting, praying, walking a labyrinth, worshiping using music from Taizé, and/or studying together. By the end of that period, in most churches, there would be a genuine spiritual awakening. There also would be a new awareness of what is really important and an openness to reconsidering how the congregation invests its time and energy.

While conflicts will still occur because what is being changed is important and treasured, the disagreements are much less likely to be destructive when you have prayed together and heard one another's prayers as everyone earnestly seeks the will and wisdom of God. Sitting in silence and seeking the Spirit is a powerful reminder that we do not rely on our own wisdom, education, and experience alone. In the tender work of sensing the gentle breath of the Spirit, a migrant worker may be more skilled than a federal judge. In what other setting would one find the humility to listen to others with respect and grace?

At the end of this book are two small group exercises. They are not designed to lead the congregation through a study of the chapters of this book. Most of the material contained in this book is designed for leaders of the congregation and would be of little interest to those who are seeking simply to worship God, follow Jesus, and serve compassionately. The purpose of the exercises is to help as many people as possible in your congregation synchronize their hearts with the heart of God. By working through the same spiritual exercises together, the entire congregation hopefully will find a new openness to permitting, and even helping, the church to be born again as a vibrant and vital body doing the work of Jesus in your community. Leaders need their prayers, their patience, and their support. Leaders also need to take this spiritual journey with them. For this reason, every leader should be engaged in one of the small groups. This may mean that the staff and their partners gather one night a week to do the study. It might be better for the leadership to be in a group with others, not leading the group but journeying as one with the group.

The first step, of course, is to train the group leaders. Recruit the number of leaders that will be needed so that 75 percent of your congregation can participate. This may mean having groups meet at odd times or at times when childcare is available. After you have recruited the leaders, ask them to recruit an assistant or apprentice. The idea is that you train enough small group leaders for the future as the church and number of groups grow. Some of the groups will want to continue, and that should be encouraged.

It often is easiest to start these groups as a Lenten discipline. It makes sense to ask everyone to gather to study and pray together following the model of the early church and in preparation for Easter. The ultimate goal is spiritual resurrection for the congregation and rebirth for the church.

In addition to the studies we have provided, there are dozens of excellent ones that will serve you well. What is critical is to provide the spiritual underpinnings for the work of change.

Prayer and fasting are important spiritual disciplines, but so is celebration. Don't forget that you gather every Sunday for the express purpose of celebrating the transforming work of God in the world and in human lives. Name this process as one of the ways in which God is expressly working in your midst. Give thanks, and don't be afraid to name what is going on inside of you. While this is not about you, it is important for people to see that the leadership is fully sharing this experience — anxieties, hopes, and joys.

Don't Forget and Don't Let the Congregation Forget That Transformation Is the Point of the Christian Faith

As the church works its way through the lectionary and liturgical cycle, it is remarkable to note how much of it speaks to renewal, change, and transformation. It is, after all, what Jesus came to do. While we progressives generally avoid the word "repent" because of its abuses, we must not forget that, ultimately, it is a word of good news. The idea that we can, and that our congregations can, repent is the ultimate testimony to both the faithfulness and grace of God. All of us know we need to make changes in our lives. We don't need to beat people up to persuade them to be different. What we do need to do is offer them the opportunity to become the people they have always dreamed they could be — to repent, change directions, be transformed. That it is possible is the great good news of the redeeming grace of God.

Kirk Hadaway reminds us that the late social ecologist and business guru Peter Drucker, who was also a man of faith, said, "The business of the church is to change people; the business of a corporation is to satisfy them." I would add that churches that get that backward die, and should. Churches that exist to satisfy their members have become closed clubs neglecting the mission of Jesus. Like the Dead Sea that seeks to retain all the water that flows into it, soon all life ceases to exist.

Transcendent worship, spiritual formation in community, and sharing one's self in service of compassion are all means by which the church is a catalyst for transformation. If people leave our worship unchanged then we need to change our worship. If people are not transformed in small groups then we need to give birth to different kinds of small groups. If the service ministries of our church aren't changing people's lives then we need to find people with profound needs and learn from them.

Making changes in a church is hard work. Transforming religious people is so difficult it killed Jesus. It is possible though. You and I aren't the people we hope to be, but we aren't the people we once were either. We are different because we learned something, were deeply and repeatedly moved, met some people and became known by them, and were given an opportunity to help, give, and serve. These are the ways people are changed. Sometimes pain is the motivator, but pain and even the threat of death don't transform the human soul. That is a spiritual process, and the ministry of the church is to help people go through that process in the same way Jesus did:

- He told them the truth and challenged them to change.
- He taught them and encouraged them.
- He led them into the presence of God.
- He gathered them into community and had them grow together.
- He sent them out to help and heal.
- He gave them hope of resurrection.

If the church can be the Body of Christ in these ways not only will it be transformed, it will be once more a transforming power in the world. Thanks be to God.

Pilgrim Churches Small Group Study

PILGRIM CHURCHES
SESSION ONE: HOSPITALITY

Icebreaker

What was your first visit to our church like?

Scripture

Have a different group member read each of the following scripture passages aloud:

- Romans 15:7
- Matthew 25:31–40
- Deuteronomy 10:19
- Hebrews 13:2
- Romans 12:9–13

Discussion

1. All of these references encourage us to practice hospitality. Within the context of a worship service, how would you define hospitality? Is it just being friendly, or is there more to it? Why is hospitality a core value for Christians? What are the limits to hospitality?

2. Who invited you to church the first time? What activities or ministries made you feel "at home"? What didn't? What can our church do to welcome newcomers more concretely?

3. Imagine you're a first-time visitor to our church. As you arrive at the building, what do you find welcoming and what obstacles do you encounter? Do you know where to go? Is the worship space clean and cared for? Are restrooms clearly marked? How would parents with small children react? What about disabled folks? Is there close parking available? Who's available to offer directions and answer questions?

4. At church do you see yourself as a host or a guest? What are the responsibilities of a host?

5. When was the last time you invited a friend to attend a worship service? What prevents you from inviting friends to church? What have you found here that someone else needs?

6. In her book *Christianity for the Rest of Us*, Diana Butler Bass sums up how hospitality is a core Christian value:

> True Christian hospitality is not a recruitment strategy designed to manipulate strangers into church membership. Rather, it is a central practice of the Christian faith — something Christians are called to do for the sake of that thing itself.... Christians welcome strangers as we ourselves have been welcomed into God through the love of Jesus Christ. Through hospitality, Christians imitate God's welcome. Therefore, hospitality is not a program, not a single hour or ministry in the life of a congregation. It stands at the heart of a Christian way of life, a living icon of wholeness in God.
>
> Given this expansive understanding of hospitality, how does this value get lived out beyond the church walls? For example, how does Christian hospitality inform our attitudes toward the homeless? Toward immigrants?

Prayer Requests

Have each group member share a prayer request regarding how they might integrate hospitality into their Christian life and practice. How might we all become hosts instead of guests?

PILGRIM CHURCHES
SESSION TWO: DISCERNMENT

Icebreaker

Begin with a group exercise that everyone can do. Invite everyone to get comfortable, still their minds, close their eyes, and listen to the silence for sixty seconds. *The truth is that the world we live in is rarely silent. Notice how many different sounds you actually are hearing. Count them.* After about thirity more seconds, invite them to open their eyes. How many sounds had they noticed? List them.

Scripture (1 Kings 19:1–13)

Background: This passage follows Elijah's great defeat of the prophets of Baal. At the moment of his greatest triumph, Queen Jezebel threatens his life, and Elijah, feeling vulnerable, flees in fear. His flight takes him into the wilderness where he complains to God about his mistreatment and announces that he wants to die, which is an interesting response from someone fleeing the threat of death. Of course, Elijah's life and ministry are not finished, so what we read in this passage is that moment of renewal when, out of victory, fear, and dejection, Elijah hears from God again.

Discussion

1. What is the meaning of the phrase "the sound of sheer silence"? What experiences does it call to mind? How does it feel to you?

2. We are noisy people. We talk a lot and fill those moments when we are not talking with music, or news, or sports,

or. . . . Why? Are we afraid of silence? Is it like when we were kids and were afraid of the dark? We didn't know what was there, and we were afraid that whatever it was would grab us, take us, or hurt us. Now we are afraid of silence . . . Oh, we don't say that, but we manage to fill all of our waking moments with sound. So we must be afraid of something.

    a. Why are people often afraid of silence?

    b. What do we do to avoid silence?

    c. Why are *you* afraid of silence?

Exercise

The answer to "Why?" is probably complex, but let me pose another question for us to ponder. What if what we fear in the silence is hearing the question that God asked Elijah: "What are you doing here?"

Let's try another experiment with silence. I want you to get comfortable and close your eyes again. This time, we are going to be silent for five minutes, and during that time I want you to meditate on the Elijah question: "What are you doing here?" At the end of every minute, I will read the question again, and, if your mind has wandered, let the question call you back. Ready? Close your eyes and see if you can hear the Spirit calling you by name and asking, "What are you doing here?"

After the time is done, give people an opportunity to share anything they want to about the experience. Assure them that they do not have to share anything, because those moments were between them and God, but, if they are comfortable, sharing might help the group see their common journey. After this time, offer this observation:

The practice of spiritual discernment is about learning to replace "I" questions with "God" questions. It no longer is "what do I want," or "what do I need," or "where am I going," but "what does God want," "what is God saying," "where is God going?"

If everyone will get comfortable, let's close our eyes, focus on our breathing, and see if we can sense the presence of the holy in our midst. Let us pray together silently.

After a full two minutes of silence, invite the group to let the Spirit bring to mind what is going on in our culture to which we should pay attention. Then allow for another two minutes of silence.

Discussion

1. What in our world today is breaking the heart of God? What is delighting God's heart?

2. Because we are so inundated with information, it is easy to get the impression that the latest crisis in some celebrity's life is the most important event taking place in the world today. Depending on what spin your particular favorite news source puts on events, you may think the world is headed toward Armageddon or that the Reign of God has come on earth today. It also is different if we hear negative news most loudly or if we are most influenced by good news. Our own values, experiences, and internal wiring shape our worldviews. We may be the reincarnation of our parents' values, or we may be living in radical reactions to them. There are many factors shaping how we discern the times in which we live. These factors are neither right nor wrong, good nor bad, but we need at least to be aware of them. The question is how can the whisper of God's Spirit overcome any, let alone all, of those factors in such a way that our worldview is transformed? Can you think of an example of an issue about which God has completely changed your mind over the years? Abortion? Women pastors? Gay marriage? The Bible? Health care?

Prayer Requests

For their prayer request this week, ask each person to identify an issue about which the Spirit is nudging them to grow or change.

PILGRIM CHURCHES
SESSION THREE: ART AND BEAUTY

Icebreaker

Have you ever experienced "beauty" in a worship service? What was that like?

Scripture (Exodus 25:1–18)

Background: After the Israelites are delivered from Egypt, Moses goes up to Mt. Sinai to hear God's instructions for the nation. Exodus chapters 25–27 give an exhaustive, and exhausting, summary of how the tabernacle is to be constructed, within which the tablets of the covenant are to be stored. Listen to the excerpts for creating this costly and extravagant dwelling place for God:

- Exodus 25:23–24
- Exodus 25:31
- Exodus 26:31–33

Discussion

1. Why do you think God calls for costly gold and silver for building the tabernacle? What will this tabernacle communicate to the people? What will the people experience when they encounter it? Is this extravagance for the benefit of God or the people worshiping God?

2. How important are beauty and art to a worship space? In what ways do they enhance the worship experience?

3. Protestant worship often is centered on the sermon (the spoken word), which connects with our left brain activities (reasoning, analysis, rational thought). Art, music, and

beauty speak to our right brain functioning (creativity, emotion, intuition). Is one approach preferable? Are both needed? Which allows you to more fully experience the presence of God?

4. How do you rate the typical worship experience in your church? Is it geared more to the head or to the heart?

Scripture (Luke 7:36–50)
Discussion

5. What does this passage communicate about an extravagant act of beauty?

6. A young associate pastor entered his prestigious Gothic church and admired the beautiful stained glass, thundering organ, soaring architecture, and resplendent paraments. He wondered aloud if the massive expense of this building would not have been put to better use by providing meals and clothing for the poor. His older mentor commented that this extravagance created a place where countless Christians had worshiped and been transformed by the awe-inspiring surroundings. These Christians had been transformed, emotionally as well as intellectually, to then provide the services to the poor that the young associate had proposed. Moreover, that church would continue their ministry for years based on the investment in art and beauty made years ago.

Which viewpoint makes the most sense?

Prayer Requests

Ask each member to pray for an increased sensitivity to experiencing God this week through art and beauty. Have them report back next week what they learned.

PILGRIM CHURCHES
SESSION FOUR: JUSTICE

Icebreaker

What was "keeping the Sabbath" like when you were growing up?

Scripture (Mark 3:1–6)

Discussion

1. Jews were instructed to "remember the Sabbath day, and keep it holy," which meant to refrain from any kind of work. Why do you think curing the sick would be considered work?

2. What was the agenda for Jesus in this passage? What was the Pharisees' agenda?

3. What were the Pharisees so frightened of that they wanted to have Jesus killed?

4. How does Jesus' question reframe the argument from religious rules to principles of justice? How often do you see rules and regulations get in the way of the basic principle behind them?

5. Are Christians called to be champions for justice? Why or why not?

6. What was Jesus' method for challenging an unjust rule? What emotions were involved in his action?

7. How can Christians today challenge injustice?

8. What might be the consequences for challenging injustice? Would you be willing to suffer the consequences even if you never saw the injustice corrected?

9. As a Christian, what injustices in the world grieve you the most? What are you willing to do about it?

Prayer Requests

Ask each member to share a prayer request regarding justice this week, perhaps asking to be more attuned to injustices in daily life, or having the courage to act, or the wisdom to know how best to act.

PILGRIM CHURCHES
SESSION FIVE: DIVERSITY

Icebreaker

What is your religious background?

Scripture (Romans 12:4–8)
Discussion

1. What diversity of spiritual gifts do you see in your church? Are some gifts valued more highly than others? What point is the Apostle Paul making here?

2. Do you see your congregation as theologically diverse or fairly uniform? What are the advantages of theological diversity? What are the drawbacks?

Scripture (Galatians 3:28)
Discussion

3. How would you describe your congregation's diversity in terms of age, race, gender, socio-economic status, sexual orientation, long-term members vs. relatively new members?

4. Is diversity valued or avoided? Why?

5. What is the difference between tolerance and appreciation? Does your church typically tolerate or appreciate differences in members? How is that demonstrated?

6. Mentally select a demographic group with which you have little in common. How would you react if a few from this group occasionally attended worship services at

your church? If a large number from this group started attending worship services regularly? If they started assuming leadership positions in your church?

7. What's the difference between diversity as a Christian value and politically correct multiculturalism? How are each lived out?

8. Does valuing diversity mean you have to accept everybody, all the time, with no reservations?

Prayer Requests

Have each member share a personal prayer request regarding an area where God is calling them to grow.

PILGRIM CHURCHES
SESSION SIX: ONE PLANET, ONE CHANCE

Icebreaker

Have you ever had a "religious experience" in nature?

Scripture (Psalm 148)
Discussion

1. What is the writer's view of the natural world?

2. How do inanimate objects like the moon and stars "praise God?"

3. How are humans related to creation in this psalm?

4. If we regard creation as the psalmist did, how will that affect how we treat creation?

Scripture (Leviticus 25:1–5)
Discussion

5. God gave these instructions to the Israelites before they entered the Promised Land. How did these commands define who really owned the land that they would be entering?

6. "Stewardship" is a word we usually connect with putting money into the offering plate, but it actually means "taking care of things not our own." How do these commands in Leviticus express good stewardship of the earth?

Scripture (Matthew 6:25–34)

Discussion

7. How do Jesus' words from the Sermon on the Mount express the same spirit as the commands in Leviticus?

8. What is the relationship between worry and exploitation of resources?

9. What causes you the most worry?

10. These scriptures all were directed to people living in an agricultural society. How can these principles be applied to the use of resources in our world today?

Prayer Requests

Have each member identify one environmental concern for which God may be leading them to take action.

APPENDIX B

Pilgrim People Small Group Study

PILGRIM PEOPLE
SESSION ONE: PRAYER

Icebreaker

What is the first prayer you ever learned?

Scripture (Matthew 6:5–13)
Discussion

1. What is prayer? Is it talking and listening? What percentage of time do you spend talking to God vs. listening to God?

2. How do you listen to God? In what ways can you hear God speak to you?

3. What does it mean to pray "your will be done"? Do we really mean it when we pray the Lord's Prayer?

4. What warnings about prayer does Jesus offer in this passage?

5. If God knows your needs before you pray, what's the point of telling God about them?

6. What happens exactly when you pray? Do you change God's mind, does God change your circumstances, or does God change you?

Scripture (1 Thessalonians 5:16–22)
Discussion

7. What does it mean to "pray without ceasing"?

8. What does a life centered in prayer look like?

Prayer Requests

Ask each participant to share a personal concern for which the other members might pray for them in the coming week. The prayer request should be brief and personal. Have each person covenant to pray for each member and their needs on the list each day.

PILGRIM PEOPLE
SESSION TWO: PRESENCE

Icebreaker

What was the most memorable meal you've ever had?

Scripture (Luke 4:14–19)

Discussion

1. In Luke's Gospel, this story is the account of Jesus' inaugural address, in which he begins his public ministry. Notice that Jesus went to the synagogue "as was his custom." Is regular worship a custom for you?

2. What motivates you to get up and come to church on a Sunday morning? Is it habit? A desire to see church friends? An obligation or sense of duty? Guilt? An expectation of encountering God? All of these?

3. In the average church, 70 percent of the congregation is present at worship 75 percent of the time. How often do you attend worship? What are we missing when we miss church?

4. Imagine all the meals you have consumed over the course of your life. What percentage of those was memorable? Most meals, like worship services, are routine, yet they all provide nourishment. How are our souls malnourished when we skip church?

5. What do we gain by attending worship? How does focusing on the eternal affect our lives? Is worshiping in

community more powerful than private devotion? Why or why not?

Prayer Requests

Ask each participant to share a brief personal prayer request. Have each member also pray daily for next week's worship service: for those leading worship, for any first-time visitors, and for an effective service in which people can have a powerful encounter with God.

PILGRIM PEOPLE
SESSION THREE: SERVICE

Icebreaker

In what ways have you volunteered your time and energy for the benefit of others?

Scripture (John 13:1–17)

Discussion

1. In this story, Jesus models the idea of "servant leadership." How would you define this term?

2. How do you think Jesus' disciples reacted to this lesson?

3. What are the benefits to serving others?

4. A bio-feedback experiment was done with groups of college students. They were connected to machines that measured their responses. The two groups were shown different videos. The first group saw video tapes of beautiful vacation spots: pristine white-sand beaches, cottages on the marsh, cabins in the Smokey Mountains. The researchers noted that the viewers' stress level dropped dramatically. Their pulse slowed, their muscles relaxed.

   The second group saw a tape of the staff and volunteers in a hospital that cared for terminally ill patients. The average stay in this hospital was twenty-six days and patients left only when they died. The students were visibly moved by the caring of the volunteers and staff. The machines registered that, biologically, their response was much the same as with the first film. Their stress seemed to drain as they saw people with needs much greater than theirs and as they saw one human caring for another.

The one difference the researchers noted was that in the second group endorphins were present in the bloodstream at a much higher level than in the first group. Endorphins are chemical cousins to medications like morphine. Just watching people serving gave them a natural high.

Have you ever experienced a natural high for helping someone else?

5. What are the pitfalls of serving others? How do you feel about trying to serve someone who takes advantage of you? Are we justified in not helping people at times? Is it worth the gamble to help someone even when she might abuse the help?

Prayer Requests

Ask each member to share a personal prayer request with the group. Also, have each participant pray that God will identify an opportunity to serve in Christ's name this week.

PILGRIM PEOPLE
SESSION FOUR: GENEROSITY

Icebreaker

What motivates you to donate money, time, or your service?

Scripture (Malachi 3:8–10)
Discussion

1. What is a tithe? Is a literal 10 percent still the expectation for Christians today?

2. Americans earning less than $25,000 per year contribute an average of 4.2 percent of their household income to charitable groups, while those making $100,000 or more donate an average 2.7 percent. How would you explain this difference?

3. How does not giving to God equate to robbing God? Does God need your offering, or do you need to give it?

4. This passage promises overflowing blessings poured down from heaven. What sort of blessings do you receive when you are generous? What do you miss out on when you are not generous?

5. If God is the source of all that we have, is returning a tithe an obligation, a reasonable expectation, or an opportunity to express gratitude?

6. What does tithing teach us about priorities?

Prayer Request

Ask each member to share a personal prayer request with the group. Also, have each participant pray for a chance to exhibit generosity this week.

PILGRIM PEOPLE
SESSION FIVE: SPIRITUAL GROWTH

Icebreaker

What was your view of God when you were a child?

Scripture (1 Peter 2:1–10)
Discussion

1. What does it mean to be a "living stone"? To be "built into a spiritual house"?

2. Do we as Christians typically see ourselves as "a chosen race, a royal priesthood, a holy nation"? If we did how would we live differently?

3. Those who show up in church on Sunday often can be categorized in one of two ways:

    a. Tourists: those who are spiritual but not religious; those who are shopping for a church home; those who tend to be spectators rather than participants; those who are observers but are not invested.

    b. Pilgrims: those who have committed their lives, even though they may not have all the answers; those whose faith is moving, growing, and maturing; those who engage in spiritual practices that foster growth.

    How do you rate your congregation: what percentage are tourists, pilgrims, or somewhere in between? How do you rate yourself?

4. How can we move from being tourists to pilgrims? What spiritual disciplines can help?

Prayer Requests

Ask the members to choose a new spiritual discipline that they can start this week.

Bibliography

Bass, Diana Butler. *Christianity for the Rest of Us: How the Neighborhood Church Is Transforming the Faith.* New York: HarperOne, 2007.

———. *The Practicing Congregation: Imagining a New Old Church.* Herndon, Va.: Alban Institute, 2004.

Block, Peter. *Stewardship: Choosing Service Over Self-Interest.* San Francisco: Barret-Koehler Publishers, 1996.

Bowman, Ray, and Eddie Hall. *When Not to Build: An Architect's Unconventional Wisdom for the Growing Church.* Grand Rapids, Mich.: Baker Books, 2000.

Butler, Phil. *Well Connected: Releasing Power, Restoring Hope through Kingdom Partnerships.* Colorado Springs, Colo.: Authentic, 2005.

Cole, Neil. *Church 3.0: Upgrades for the Future of the Church.* San Francisco: Jossey-Bass, 2010.

Collins, Jim. *Good to Great: Why Some Companies Make the Leap . . . and Others Don't.* New York: HarperBusiness, 2001.

Cooke, Phil. *Branding Faith: Why Some Churches and Non-profits Impact Culture and Others Don't.* Ventura, Calif.: Regal, 2008.

Dawn, Marva. *Reaching Out without Dumbing Down: A Theology of Worship for These Urgent Times.* Grand Rapids, Mich.: Wm. B. Eerdmans, 1995.

de Bono, Edward. *I Am Right and You are Wrong: From This to the New Renaissance: From Rock Logic to Water Logic.* New York: Penguin Books, 1992.

Easum, William M. *Sacred Cows Make Gourmet Burgers: Ministry Anytime, Anywhere, By Anyone.* Nashville: Abingdon Press, 1995.

Foss, Michael W. *Power Surge: Six Marks of Discipleship for a Changing Church.* Minneapolis: Augsburg Fortress Publishers, 2000.

Gerber, Michael E. *The E-Myth Revisited: Why Most Small Businesses Don't Work and What to Do About It.* New York: HarperCollins, 2001.

Gibbs, Eddie, and Ryan Bolger. *Emerging Churches: Creating Christian Community in Postmodern Cultures.* Grand Rapids, Mich.: Baker Academic, 2005.

Gifford, Mary Louise. *The Turnaround Church: Inspiration and Tools for Life-Sustaining Change.* Herndon, Va.: Alban Institute, 2009.

Greenleaf, Robert K. *The Servant as Leader.* Westfield, Ind.: Greenleaf Center for Servant Leadership, 1970.

Hadaway, C. Kirk. *Behold I Do a New Thing: Transforming Communities of Faith.* Cleveland: Pilgrim Press, 2001.

Hamm, Richard. *Recreating the Church: Leadership in the Postmodern Age.* Danvers, Mass.: Chalice Press, 2007.

Hart, Ted, James M. Greenfield, and Michael Johnston. *Non-Profit Internet Strategies — Best Practices for Marketing, Communications and Fundraising.* Hoboken, N.J.: John Wiley & Sons, 2005.

Hart, Ted, James M. Greenfield and Sheeraz D. Haji. *People to People Fundraising: Social Networking and Web 2.0 for Charities.* Hoboken, N.J.: John Wiley & Sons, 2007.

Jones, Laurie Beth. *Jesus, CEO: Using Ancient Wisdom for Visionary Leadership.* New York: Hyperion, 1995.

Kinnaman, David, and Gabe Lyons. *Unchristian: What a New Generation Really Thinks about Christianity . . . and Why It Matters.* Grand Rapids, Mich.: Baker Books, 2007.

Kotter, John P. *Leading Change.* Boston: Harvard Business School Press, 1996.

Herrington, Jim, James Furr, and Mike Bonem. *Leading Congregational Change: A Practical Guide for the Transformational Journey.* Hoboken, N.J.: John Wiley & Sons, 2000.

Maxwell, John C. *The 21 Irrefutable Laws of Leadership: Follow Them and People Will Follow You.* Nashville: Thomas Nelson, 1998.

McLoughlin, William G. *Revivals, Awakenings and Reform: An Essay on Religion and Social Change in America, 1607–1977.* Chicago: University of Chicago Press, 1978.

McNeal, Reggie. *Missional Renaissance: Changing the Scorecard for the Church.* San Francisco: Jossey-Bass, 2009.

Pagitt, Doug. *Church in the Inventive Age.* Minneapolis: Sparkhouse Press, 2010.

Putnam, Robert D. *Bowling Alone: The Collapse and Revival of American Community.* New York: Simon & Schuster, 2000.

Reising, Richard L. *Church Marketing 101: Preparing Your Church for Greater Growth.* Grand Rapids, Mich.: Baker Books, 2006.

Rendle, Gil, and Alice Mann. *Holy Conversations: Strategic Planning as a Spiritual Practice for Congregations.* Herndon, Va.: Alban Institute, 2004.

Schnase, Robert. *Five Practices of Fruitful Congregations.* Nashville: Abingdon Press, 2007.

Senge, Peter M. *The Fifth Discipline: The Art and Practice of the Learning Organization.* New York: Doubleday, 2006.

Shih, Clara. *The Facebook Era: Tapping Online Social Networks to Market, Sell, and Innovate.* Upper Saddle River, N.J.: Prentice Hall, 2010

Spears, Larry C. *Reflections on Leadership: How Robert K. Greenleaf's Theory of Servant-Leadership Influenced Today's Top Management Thinkers.* New York: John Wiley & Sons, 1995.

Standish, N. Graham. *Becoming a Blessed Church: Forming a Church of Spiritual Purpose, Presence, and Power.* Herndon, Va.: Alban Institute, 2005.

Stevens, Tim, and Tony Morgan. *Simply Strategic Stuff: Help for Leaders Drowning in the Details of Running a Church.* Loveland, Colo.: Group Publishing, 2004.

Thistlethwaite, Susan Brooks. *Dreaming of Eden: American Religion and Politics in a Wired World.* New York: Palgrave Macmillan, 2005.

Tickle, Phyllis. *The Great Emergence: How Christianity Is Changing and Why.* Grand Rapids, Mich.: Baker Books, 2008.

Warren, Michael, ed. *Changing Churches: The Local Church and the Structures of Change.* Portland, Ore.: Pastoral Press, 2000.

Warwick, Mal. *Fundraising When Money Is Tight: A Strategic and Practical Guide to Surviving Tough Times and Thriving in the Future.* San Francisco: Jossey-Bass, 2009.

Warwick, Mal, Ted Hart, and Nick Allen, eds. *Fundraising on the Internet — The ePhilanthropy Foundation.org's Guide to Success Online.* San Francisco: Jossey-Bass, 2002.